7 Ingredients To An Effective Prayer Life

7 Ingredients To An Effective Prayer Life

COMPILED BY
Trena D Stephenson

PUBLISHER
Daughters of Distinction

7 Ingredients To An Effective Prayer Life
Published by Daughters of Distinction
PO Box 9001
Silver Spring, Maryland 20906

Copyright @2013 DOFDLLC
Daughters of Distiniction

All rights reserved. No part of the book may be reproduced in any form without permission in writing from the publisher, except in case of brief quotations embodied in articles or reviews

Cover Design: Deborah Settles
Editorial: Cynthia D. Thomas

PREFACE

Seven Ingredients to an Effective Prayer Life
Volumes 6 & 7

It's always exciting when God causes people to come together to fulfill His mandate and purpose for a Kingdom assignment. Truly, the revealed will of His Ruach (spirit) is released as a sound in the each person as they seek to accomplish His will in the earth. Prayer is the essential Key to maintaining strategy in the Kingdom of Heaven and in the Earth. Jesus says to the Disciples in the Gospel according to St. Matthew 16:19 "And I will give unto thee the keys of the Kingdom of heaven." Keys represent ingredients to the recipe of the power to unlock or release authority to everyone who follows (obeys) the recipe given in detail. In each volume of this powerful collaboration (book), it gives essential details of the recipe. After reading the first two series, it was imperative to finish the entire book collection with this final accumulation. In these volumes, you will find that the authors have spoken to each area to provide an understanding of what the Holy Spirit is saying to them. This will help to inspire you as a reader to follow and maintain a more active prayer life. The footnote of Matthew 16:19 speak to binding (forbidding) and loosing (permitting).

Oftentimes, people misuse this authority given to them; it's either they don't use it or they use it in the wrong way. These abilities were given to the kingdom citizens as spiritual access to the Kingdom of

Heaven, so it can be released on earth. If we just take a moment to review the chapter on "honesty ", we can see it speaks to the whole heart of the matter.

This chapter will cause you to speak to God from a place of truth and not with selfish motives. Prayer without honesty is not prayer; it's another form of disobedience or in my opinion a vain representation of selfish murmuring. Then there is the chapter on the Fruits of the Spirit, to which I can only say, wow! Understand that love is the key to every prayer released to Heaven. In this chapter, the writer speaks to the Spirit of Love, which deals with importance of the desire of the person; as they seek God for the answer through prayer, once again not having a selfish desire. Beloved, this entire series of books was written for you from the heart of God. Apostle Trena Stephenson, along with each anointed author, including yours truly, penned each chapter with the heart of God; speaking to the believer to help fortify their prayer life, thus giving each reader, the Ingredients to an Effective Prayer Life.

Serving as the primary leader for the body of Christ for over twenty years, I am richly blessed after reading this book series. As a Chief Apostle, serving many of the clarion leaders around the globe, I have recommended that each leader infuse their congregations with the book series. To you the readers, as a professional theologian, this book is sound to the idea of Christ method for the body of Christ as it relates to the art of prayer. You will find that this book will change your way of thinking and help to improve your prayer life. To every intercessor, this book is a must have in your library.

To every pastor it is a must to be used for your leadership and Christian education ministry. To every believer, you will find yourself in this book series. What can I say? You will never be the same after reading this book series.

These final volumes are a must have to complete the series. It is similar to baking a cake. You must be sure it doesn't fall or taste funny, to do that it is always good to follow the recipe. You must pay close attention to the details, mixing in each ingredient to complete the recipe. Be sure to follow this book series and buy this final book, it is soul filling and inspirational to the reader. This book is a life-giving tool; an excellent spiritual guide for everyone desires to have an Effective Prayer Life. Once again, job well done to Apostle Trena Stephenson, all authors and contributors to this entire book series. In addition, to every reader watch God take your Prayer Life to the Place of Effective..........

Shalom

By His Grace I am:

Dr. William Billups D.Min.
Chief Apostle and International Presiding Prelate
Manifest Kingdom Global Presidium and Allied Bodies

FOREWORD

"Seven Ingredients to an Effective Prayer Life (Volumes Six through Seven)" is very interesting reading. The book's purpose is to teach people the ingredients for an effective prayer life. It is my pleasure to provide foreword and to recommend this book. The disciples asked Jesus to teach them how to pray and He said to them pray saying "Our Father…" in the prayer Jesus taught the disciples. The ingredients to an effective prayer life are learned by doing and practicing, not just by reading. We need to develop a persistent prayer life as mentioned in the book.

Children reveal the kind of humility we should have in approaching God as "Our Father." Jesus loved children because of the child like faith. We can learn a lot from children. They are not anxious about anything but believe that God will answer their prayers. This point is illustrated when Jesus asked the disciples, which father among you would give a snake to your son who asked for a fish? (Luke 11:11). How much more will the Heavenly Father give the Holy Spirit to those who ask him? I recommend you read this book which provides a road map of how to have an effective prayer life.

Dad of Apostle Trena D. Stephenson
CEO of Daughters of Distinction LLC

Rev. Charles E. Jackson
Pastor of Mount Bethel United Methodist Church
McDonough, Georgia

TABLE OF CONTENTS
VOLUME VI FRUIT OF THE SPIRIT

Spirit of Love	11
Spirit of Joy	17
Peace, Be Still	24
The Fruit of the Spirit - Patience	30
The Parable of an Answer to a Consistent and Effectual Prayer Life: "A Prophetic Blueprint Revealed in the Ingredient GOOD"	40
Maintaining "Faithfulness" A "Prepared" Package	51
The Fruits of the Spirit - Humbleness and Self Control "A True and Faithful Servant"	62

CHAPTER 1

Spirit of Love

What is love? Many of us today are still living our lives trying to figure out what love is? Let's start with the definition of love , A strong affection for another arising out of kinship or personal ties for example maternal love for a child.

How many of you have dated and all you could think about was the love that you had for this mate and all they did was let you down? How often did you feel like you gave your all and you got nothing in return? Well, the combining equation to your ongoing problem was that you trusted all your love into the wrong thing. You have to learn how to love God before you can learn to love man.

I had this same problem time after time again. I spent countless seconds, minutes, hours, days and years trying to be the perfect love to not only my mate but my family, as well. I just knew that giving my mom, dad, sister and brothers everything that their hearts desired, I would in return receive endless love. Unfortunately it took many disappointing situations to know that giving my all to someone when it wasn't my season would sow nothing but heartbreak. So, of course when I started to date I looked for those types of men who needed me. Men I could count on to need me to rescue them out of every downfall. Why was this I wonder? Because I didn't have Jesus in my life and neither did my mate. I hadn't yet realized that I was trying to fill a void with something. I didn't even have the slightest idea, which ingredients were missing.

Fasting forward to a time after I met my truest love, Jesus Christ. When our relationship began I wasn't sure if I could love Him unconditionally because I had been hurt so many times. I wasn't sure that my soul could handle it but I began to date Him. We would date a few Sundays a month and of course whenever I went to my auntie's house. She always invited Him to dinner with us. Aunt Dot and I would talk about my life being so disrespectful and hurtful to Jesus. I, of course, heard that premarital sex and shacking was not what God had planned for my life but I was in love with a man I knew would be my husband and no one could tell me anything different. That was of course until my boyfriend Jesus showed up and showed out!

In 2004, I gave birth to my first child out of wedlock Khalil and again I just dated Jesus one day a week. I was still trying to see if this love thing was going to work out for me my way. After a few years of verbal abuse I was tired. I figured my way wasn't going to work especially since it hadn't helped anyone else that I knew at the time either. So, I had a talk with Jesus. Again, He was there for me. He welcomed me into His home once again and this time I promised that I would definitely try His way now.

Jesus and I began to have this wonderful relationship. We would sit and talk all day. We spoke the first thing in the morning, during snack and lunch breaks and during my travel to and from home, although I still had a partial mind of my own. He was always right there telling me yes or no before I made any decision that could jeopardize our beautiful relationship. He began to shed light on me and my past and future. He began to show me what it was He wanted me to do in life. He began to show me how I could finally feel loved without having a man in the flesh to validate me. I then started to understand Him clearer. I began to read the bible and make Him priority in my life. After this, I promise my life changed for the best.

I did not want to fantasize for this perfect mate or spouse anymore. I learned that Jesus would bless me with the perfect man for me when the time came. I learned that my struggles and good heart was all a part of the plan for my life. I am one of those people who learn a lot from others mistakes. I try hard to enlighten others of those mistakes, so that they won't have to live them. This is why we are here today, so that my lessons can be a blessing to someone else. Even if just one is touched, my mission would be complete.

When we love we have to love Jesus first. He will then teach us how to love. He will teach us the real meaning of love. Jesus will teach us how to love above all other emotions and feelings. He will teach us how to love even when we feel anger is just much easier. After we begin to love Jesus where we listen to his commands and are obedient. He will then teach us how to love ourselves.

Loving ourselves is much harder than loving someone else. When you love yourself, you take time out for you. You sit down and talk to you. You listen to your thoughts and you begin to have a sense of peace in your heart. You begin to realize what things you enjoy, like and love. You begin to know you a lot better. You then are able to love someone else. Start with your family and friends. Love them unconditionally. Love them when they get on your nerves. Love them when they upset you. Love them we they listen to your problems. Love them when you all just get together to laugh and have fun. Love will become so much easier; it will be like second nature.

However, while loving don't forget to pay attention to those you love. Remember, everyone hasn't gotten their love lessons straight from Jesus. So, while loving yourself, your family and friends; you still have to love Jesus. He is the only one that will have genuine love for you every day. He loves you so much that He died on the cross for your sins, so that the mistakes that you cross in life can be a learning lesson; rather than condemnation to hell. He has to work on the love that others have for you, just as you had to work on it. Now, why is love important?

"If I have faith that can move mountains, but do not have love, I am nothing. If I give all I possess to the poor and give over my body to hardship that I may boast, but do not have love, I gain nothing. Love is patient, love is kind. It does not envy, it does not boast, it is not proud. . It does not dishonor others, it is not self-seeking, it is not easily angered, and it keeps no record of wrongs. Love does not delight in evil but rejoices with the truth. It always protects always trust, always hopes, always preserves. Love never fails." (**I Corinthians 13:2-8 New International Version NIV**). *"The three that still remains is faith, hope and love. The greatest being Love."* (**I Corinthians 13:13 NIV**)

<u>Prayer</u>

Lord, I come to You in the name of Jesus, asking You to bless us with

Your grace today. Lord, I know that throughout my life I haven't always followed Your will on time. I know that I have been naive and stubborn to Your will. I am so thankful You did not stop loving me. You held on to me until I was enlightened by Your love. I ask that You bless these readers as You have done me. I ask that You fulfill the void in their heart and souls. Lord, I ask that You hold them in your arms as You continue to teach them about love. I know that even with my few love lessons I had to learn that the reason for my forgiveness and trust and love at such a young age was because it was pure. I am blessed to have the spirit to forgive and to love. I ask that You continue to work on my love as well as those touched by these words. I ask that You continue to use me to be a blessing to others through our experiences together. Continue to teach me how to love like You love me. I thank You for this project. Lord, I surrender my heart to You. In the name of Jesus I pray, Amen!

TAKIA SMITH

Takia Smith is a member of Zion Wesley AME and the CEO of Dream Kiapers. Dream Kiapers is a non-profit organization helping young men and women with their dreams to prosper in the work force. If it means school, job or career with Kia's assistance anything is possible.

As a young woman Takia, maintained the overwhelming life of a single mom through her belief and trust in Jesus Christ. She has transformed into an awesome wife along with being a dedicated and encouraging mother of three beautiful children Khalil, Terrence and Kamille. Takia has a full time job as a DC Army National guard soldier and is a full-time college student at Strayer University. She recently received an Associate Degree in Business Management and graduated with honors. Takia would like to thank her husband Terrence, whose patience during this project was impeccable. Takia can be reached at Dreamkiapers.com, dreamkiapers@gmail.com, or dreamkiapers@facebook.com.

CHAPTER 2

Spirit of Joy

My chapter is on the Spirit of Joy. This chapter describes how to receive the spirit of joy through God's Promises. God will do what He said He will do if we stand on His word. He will come through! God did not promise me a stress free life, but He did promise if I remained faithful; He would give me joy. *"In God's presence is the fullness of joy; At His right hand are pleasures forever."* (**Psalm 16:11 New King James version NKJV**). *"Draw near to God and He will draw near to you."* (James 4:8 NKJV). *"And He said, My Presence will go with you, and I will give you rest."* (**Exodus 33:14 NKJV**). *"The LORD is near to all who call upon Him, To all who call upon Him in truth."* (**Psalm 145:18 NKJV**).

Joy Defined

Webster's New World Dictionary defines joy as synonymous with happy, glad, and cheerful. A thesaurus relates it to exultation, rapture, satisfaction, and pleasure. Webster's specifically defines it as "a very glad feeling; happiness; great pleasure; delight." It also refers to the source or cause of delight. These definitions only define the expression of the wonderful emotion. They fail to consider the causes of joy, the circumstances in which it is expressed or its longevity. In these areas, the Bible presents a much more complex virtue than these definitions indicate. I would like to share a few scriptures with you that I read that help me to discern the Spirit of Joy! In the world today, people are trying to get the fullness of joy by accumulating things. The more things you get, the more things you want. Jesus said "seek ye first the kingdom of God, and His righteousness; and all these things shall be added to you." (**Matthew 6:33 King James Version KJV**).

Solomon and Joy

King Solomon conducted a series of experiments in a quest to discover by practical experience and analysis how to get the most and best out of life. His experiments included some of the very areas just mentioned above. As Solomon described the parameters of his search for the meaning in life, he used words that are translated into English as mirth, laughter" and pleasure, all of which we normally associate with joy. Even more interesting is that the word translated as pleasure in Ecclesiastes 2:1 is the Hebrew word simha, the word most frequently translated as joy throughout the Old Testament.

"I said in my heart, "Come now, I will test you with mirth; therefore enjoy pleasure"; but surely, this also was vanity. I said of laughter— "It is madness!" and of mirth, "What does it accomplish?" I searched in my heart how to gratify my flesh with wine, while guiding my heart with wisdom, and how to lay hold on folly, till I might see what was good for the sons of men to do

under heaven all the days of their lives. I made my works great, I built myself houses, and planted myself vineyards. I made myself gardens and orchards and I planted all kinds of fruit trees in them. I made myself waterpools from which to water the growing trees of the grove. I acquired male and female servants, and had servants born in my house. Yes, I had greater possessions of herds and flocks than all who were in Jerusalem before me. I also gathered for myself silver and gold and the special treasures of kings and of the provinces, I acquired male and female singers, the delights of the sons of men, and musical instruments of all kinds. So I became great and excelled more than all who were before me in Jerusalem. Also my wisdom remained with me. Whatever my eyes desired I did not keep from them. I did not withhold my heart from any pleasure, for my heart rejoiced in all my labor; and this was my reward from all my labor. Then I looked on all the works that my hands had done and on the labor in which I had toiled; and indeed all was vanity and grasping for the wind. There was no profit under the sun." (**Ecclesiastes 2:1-11 NKJV**).

In verses 20, 22-23, 25, Solomon writes a few more conclusions after musing on several other analyses of wisdom and labor:

"Therefore I turned my heart and despaired of all the labor in which I had toiled under the sun. . . . For what has man for all his labor, and for the striving of his heart with which he had toiled under the sun? For all his days are sorrowful, and his work grievous; even in the night his heart takes no rest. This also is vanity. . . . For who can eat, or who can have enjoyment, more than I?" (**Ecclesiastes 2:20, 22-23, 25 NKJV**).

Solomon admits that his quest rewarded him with a certain

amount of joy, but he still found it unsatisfactory. We might think that with all his wealth, good health and a discerning mind, he would have had joy in abundance. What he accomplished, however, did not leave him with an enduring sense of well-being because his search continued after this experiment ended. He seems so frustrated that he says, we should seize the joy as it comes along and be content with it (Ecclesiastes 2:24). His ultimate conclusion, found in verse 26, is that God determines whether we experience joy.

What are you Pursuing During your Quest for Joy?

Does the fact that people laugh and diligently seek laughter indicate they are experiencing joy? Proverbs notes that laughter and pleasure often hide grief and sorrow (**Proverbs 14:13**). Indeed, Proverbs frequently pictures fools laughing on the road to destruction (**Proverbs 10:23; 26:19; 29:9**). Wisdom also laughs (**1:26**). Proverbs shows that the difference between the fool and the wise is the timing of laughter, its cause and its object. There is a time for laughter (**Ecclesiastes 3:4**), but Solomon's record shows that just because a person laughs does not mean he is experiencing biblical joy. Many other scriptures echo Solomon's conclusion.

Could the world have the wrong object in mind in its mad pursuit of happiness? As we saw in the previous article, biblical love is much different from this world's concept of love. Biblical love is keeping God's commandments (**I John 5:3**). It is the product, of God's Holy Spirit, shed abroad in our hearts and our yielding to its guidance. It does not arise naturally within us and frequently requires us to set our will and make sacrifices. We can see this clearly in Jesus' requirement to love our enemies.

A Christian's joy can be just as short-lived as anyone's in the world, if we are seeking it for itself as the world does. Biblical joy is a fruit, a by-product, an additional blessing; not the end in itself. It flows into and grows within the person whose life and energies are not focused merely on being joyful. The lives of those in this world that are so zealously chasing after it prove this point. If they are still chasing it, they must not yet have it. God's Word also substantiates this. We all know that joy can be expressed in many ways. Sometimes, finding joy takes time; don't expect to find it overnight. Spending meaningful time with the Lord has bought me joy, unspeakable joy, unshakable joy, everlasting joy!

<u>Prayer</u>

Father, I come to You in the name of Jesus, confessing that I have not always agreed with Your way of doing things. I admit that I have murmured and complained in this process. You have designed for my life. Lord, now I stand humbly before You trusting You to guide and sustain me during the days that lie ahead. Lord, I trust You and honor and praise Your holy name. Lord, I know You know how to get me to the place in my destiny, so I can grow as a child of God. I submit to You, and the direction You have for my life from this point forward. I choose not to get in the way of the plan You have designed for me. I realize Your way of teaching me life's lessons will far exceed my own. Teach me how to love, appreciate and cherish every moment in life. I have complete trust in Your Word and promises for me. I will obey Your instructions even when I don't understand where I am going. I declare that I am made whole by every experience I go through in life. I am free from any impairment, and I lack nothing. I commit my will to

Your plan and purpose for my life. I realize I have everything I need to succeed and become the person You ordained me to be. Before, I make any decision in life, I will seek your face in prayer. I have completely recovered from every experience in life that either came to harm me or caused me not to grow. Take my life and mold me into the person You Jesus will have me to be. Today's confession: Lord, Your will be done. Lord, do it any way You please. Thank You for allowing me to be in Your presence Lord. Please Lord, bless each reader with joy unspeakable. Amen.

As I continue this journey, I want to use every bit of my energy up on serving Him for the rest of my days. It is an honor and a privilege to write this chapter on the spirit of joy. As I look back over my life and all that God has done for me, I can truly say that I am blessed and highly favored. It brings joy right to my soul. My blessings include my two lovely daughters Darkema and Takia and my seven lovely grandchildren, Tyquan, Kemonte, Khyeema, Davonte, Khalil, Terrance and Khamil.

VERNESSA BLACKWELL

Vernessa R. Blackwell is a native of Waldorf, MD. She enlisted in the Army in 1994 and completed overseas tours to include Operation Iraqi Freedom. She is a graduate of Strayer University. Vernessa Blackwell has served in her current assignment as the S1- Operations NCO since December 2011. Among her military awards and decorations are Army Commendation (fourth award), Joint Service Commendation Medal (second Award), Army Achievement Medal (second Award), Noncommissioned Officers Development ribbon with numeral (2) National Defense Medal with Iraqi Campaign Badge. Staff Sergeant Vernessa Blackwell is divorced and the proud mother of 2 daughters, Darkema and Takia and seven wonderful grandchildren Tyquan, Kemonte, Khyeema, Davonte, Khalil, Terrence, and Kamille.

Vernessa came to know Christ in 1985. She is a member of Sanctuary of Kingdom Square. She is the proud owner of Anointed Affairs Weddings and Events founded in 1997.

CHAPTER 3

Peace, Be Still!

    I have been to the courthouse more times than I can count over the past two years. In fact, thousands of dollars have been spent for attorney's fees and plenty of nights have been sleepless because my pillows were soaked with tears. My frequent visits to the courthouse had nothing to do with my profession but due to the after effects of a bad break up. When this process first began, I never would have imagined being in this position; having to defend myself against someone that I once considered to be a friend. I blamed everyone and contrary to popular belief, I blamed myself. My self-condemnation was so bad that I would not let anyone console, encourage or pray for me because my thoughts were "I did this to myself", "I should have known better", and "I deserved this." As one could expect, these thoughts turned into what I spoke and what I did. Even with these thoughts, I made sure that I was prepared for the hearings. I had legal counsel, documented incidents, witnesses and I got everything I was asking for! I won right? Wrong! I may have won in the eyes of man but I really lost because I still did not have peace!

    The life experience I just described reminds me of the story in

Mark 4:35-41 when Jesus was in the boat with His disciples and a heavy storm came. According to the story, the storm was so heavy that the ship filled with water. During the storm, Jesus was found sleeping in the corner of the ship until He was awakened by His scared disciples asking Him if He cared if they were to drown. When Jesus arose, He rebuked the winds and said to the sea "Peace, be still."

At that point in my life, the ship was my life. It was being tossed around in with the waves of loneliness, financial distress, embarrassment and condemnation. Just like the disciples, I was worried, afraid and full of anxiety. In retrospect, just as Jesus was in the corner of the ship. He was also in my corner waiting for me to wake Him up so that He could give me peace.

The Lord showed me that one of the reasons why I did not have peace is because I never acknowledged that Jesus was peace. I've been in the church my entire life and can quote scriptures on peace, but not once did I really think that it could be applied to me. *"For to us a child is born, to us a son is given; and the government shall be upon his shoulder, and his name shall be ... Prince of Peace."* (**Isaiah 9:6 KJV**). Well, I know that I am in Him and He is in me; so, if He is peace then I shall have it!

Another area that was difficult for me to have peace was when I was being falsely accused. During those times, I've learned that in order to have peace, it was critical that I hold my peace. Holding my peace was tough as I was known to fight fire with fire and always have the last word. *"He who guards his mouth and his tongue keeps himself from calamity."* (**Proverbs 21:23 NIV**). Not holding my peace got me into a lot of trouble and did not bring forth any fruit in my life. If Jesus can hold His peace when He was being falsely accused and condemned by the Jewish council, *"But he held his peace, and answered nothing"* (**Mark 14:61 KJV**), then surely I can hold my peace.

    Peace is one of the fruits of the spirit that can truly be an armor of protection for life's circumstances. It can protect against the foolishness of man, past hurts, failures, self-doubt, worry, generational curses, unemployment, health, church hurt or even depression. Even when these matters form, they will not prosper because of being kept in "perfect peace" (**Isaiah 26: 3**). Just like Jesus said to the sea, "Peace, be still", so shall He command the storms of life. Peace will begin to rain until it overflows. Sleep will become easier because of knowing that Jesus is in the corner of the ship. "6Be anxious for nothing, but in everything by prayer and supplication with thanksgiving let your requests be made known to God. 7And the peace of God, which surpasses all comprehension, shall guard your hearts and your minds in Christ Jesus." (Philippians 4:6-7 NKJV). When peace is absent, this means that Jesus is needed even more. Peace is an essential fruit of the spirit and it is ours to have as it is mentioned over 100 times in the King James Version of the Bible. Here are other verses where it is mentioned:

    "Now may the Lord of peace himself give you peace at all times in every way. The Lord be with you all" (**II Thessalonians 3:16 NKJV**).

> *"And let the peace of Christ rule in your hearts, to which indeed you were called in one body. And be thankful."* (**Colossians 3:15 NKJV**).

> *"Peace I leave with you; my peace I give to you; not as the world

gives do I give to you. Let not your hearts be troubled, neither let them be afraid." (**John 14:27 NKJV**).

"I have said these things to you, that in me you may have peace. In the world you will have tribulation. But take heart; I have overcome the world." (**John 16:33 English Standard Version ESV**)

Let us pray…
Heavenly Father, as I seek Your face to learn more about the peace that You have for me, help me to move in spiritual boldness to command the storms in my life to be still. In the name of Jesus, I believe that Your peace will surpass all understanding and that I will stand confidently knowing Your Word to be true. This I ask in the name of Jesus, Amen.

HENNITHER BIANCA COLE

Hennither Cole is known as a Human Resources Expert, due to almost a decade of experience in recruitment, selection, compensation, and employment law experience in the non-profit, private, Fortune 500 and government sectors. Hennither has turned her set of skills into an undeniable passion for helping individuals attain  the career or business of their dreams resulting in the birth of her company Career Image Solutions, LLC where the motto is "Your Career is Our Image." Besides working with her clients, Hennither also has discovered a niche for public speaking. She has delivered countless sermons as a lay speaker for the Baltimore-Washington Conference, and former member of the local Toastmasters. She has served as a panelist for professional development college workshops and led countless community workshops for career seekers and business owners. Other accomplishments include: being a recipient of the Women of Power Award and serving as an Alternate Dispute Resolution Mediator for the Department of Defense.

Furthermore, Hennither plays an active role in the community by developing youth and adult events like "Soldiers on the Battlefield" and is the visionary for the "Step Out the Box- Women's Event."

She also mentors youth by providing assistance with their college essay submissions. Hennither is also found on the local airwaves as a contributor to the Ryan & Bryan Show. She currently serves as an expert on the show's "Corporate Ladder" segment and has been featured guest speaker on other radio programs.

CHAPTER 4

The Fruit of the Spirit

Patience

Prayer and Patience

Waiting on things can be frustrating. When we bring our concerns to the Lord, repeatedly; we grow tired of waiting. It soon begins to feel like our prayers are falling on deaf ears. Often our desire is to take control and just do the best we can and suddenly seek for other ways of gaining our desires. This is our fleshy reaction to the silence.

Galatians 5:22, lists patience as a fruit of the Holy Spirit; based on this we confess God's desire to rule our lives. It is often called longsuffering-meaning we are to keep a long and slow temper towards God, others and ourselves. This spiritual posture calls for grace. Grace compels us to trust God. We can extend grace to others when they hurt us and grace to forgive ourselves when we stumble, and fall.

This Doesn't Mean Our Circumstances Change

When we pray, we ask the Spirit to fill us, empower, and direct us even as we continue to wait on the Lord. However, we may realize that it's the same time and season one we have troubles. Our own children remain sick or are in the hospital, our marriage is stagnated, as well as, sitting on a rock, our finances are in a mess, our children are stressed; because we are unable to provide for their basic needs and the hope we have held onto for months and years fades with increasing speed. Having prayed fervently about whatever issue you are facing too many times to count; it's easy to feel your bank of patience depleting and drying once again. On these days, remember; you are not alone in the waiting.

For we know that the whole creation groans and travails in pain together until now. And not only they, but ourselves also, who have the firstfruits of the Spirit, even we ourselves groan within ourselves, waiting for the adoption, that is the redemption of our body. For we are saved by hope: but hope that is seen is not hope: for what a man sees, why does he yet hope for? But if we hope what we see not, then do we with patience wait for it." (**Romans 8:22-25 KJV**).

Waiting is a common experience to committed Christians. All your brothers and sisters in faith, as well as, all creation know what it is like to wait on the Lord. Consider, those who waited before you; Job, David, Abraham. There are plenty of examples of encouragement in the Bible concerning a need for patience. Many examples show those who have excelled at waiting. **James 5:7, Colossians 1:10-12, Psalm 40:1 and Revelation 14:12** are just a few examples of the passages about the topic

Having patience is characterized by a God given restraint in the face of opposition or oppression. Patience is only needed when there's

Daughters of Distinction

a reason to not wait. It's only necessary in the face of opposition. This is why seeking patience in many senses a battle. The promise we can lean on here is that patience is a divine restraint from God. The Lord is the one who provides us with the spiritual armor to go into battle. We often think of patience as mere endurance, but that is not true. It's more than just endurance, because we are not exercising restraint on our strength. In truth, our only responsibility is to trust that God will provide the strength; to hold on and then act accordingly to our faith in that promise.

We receive this strength by being filled with the Spirit. As Christians, we know that the ultimate source of patience is the Holy Spirit, which lives within us. We ask Him for strength to persevere in whatever situation we find ourselves. This is a provision we can claim by faith as taught to us in **Romans 5:1-5**.

The experience of waiting on God reminds us that our reality as Christians is not within our apparent circumstances, but rather in the truth of Christ's love and life in us. This gives us hope as **Romans 8:28 (KJV)** assures us that *"we know that in all things God works for the good of those who love him, who have been called according to his purpose."* It is not in our abilities to know the time or way in which God will work things out. **Ecclesiastes 3:11** and **Isaiah 55:8-9** are great reminders that these solely rest in the domain of God's knowledge. Our role here is to trust the promise of **Philippians 1: 6** and wait with hope as God brings about to completion the good work; He began in each of our lives.

What is Our Role in the Battle?

Although, God graces with divine restraint in difficult situations,

God allows us to access divine restraint; but it is our choice to accept it and act in willful obedience. Adam and Eve were given complete free will. They were gifted with many provisions in the garden; so they wouldn't need to partake in the fruit that was forbidden. However, they chose not to exercise restraint and instead disobeyed God's command. When we use God given restraint to wait on His will and timing, we renounce their fallen action actions and step out in obedience towards God.

There's Purpose in the Process

Waiting on God forces us to look to Him (**Hebrews 12:2**). It casts our eyes rightly to Christ as the source of our faith and the assurance of our salvation. It reminds us that Christ's death and life is the reason we can be filled with and empowered by the Holy Spirit. Trials cause us to persevere by deepening our knowledge of God and relying on Him more intentionally as **James 1:2-4** tells us it is here that a mature and complete faith is grown.

Standing Patiently When We Wait on the Lord Doesn't Mean Being Struck at a Standstill

Consider **Ephesians 6:10**, which instruct us to put on the full armor of God, so we can stand. When the day of evil comes, you may be able to stand your ground, and after you have done everything stand firm.

To hold your ground by remaining obedient to the Lord while waiting is not passive. Patience is an act of the will to claim ground for the kingdom of God, and is rewarded richly by Him. **Revelation 3:10-11**, tells us of God's care for those who persevere through the battle. Whether, we feel we lack patience to wait on God, or continue to love those that may be hard to love; we do have access to all the patience we need. We can trust God to give us the strength to bear the circumstances and instead use the time of waiting to grow in intimacy with the Lord.

Secondly, waiting upon the Lord doesn't mean defeat, but instead it gives God an open door to fight on our behalf. However, God needs full approval from us. When Saul failed to wait upon Him in **I Samuel 13:1-13**, it closed every avenue and landing rights for God to exercise His divine responsibility as protector of His children. On the other hand, David just trusted God even when his son, Absalom, rose against him; and indeed he was delivered (**I Samuel 15:30-31**). Realize that it's not the money, riches, wealth, and strength one has that saves, but the trust upon God and His saving power. Our victory is directly dependent on focus and the trust upon God.

Breakthrough is in the Soul

Notice that our true prosperity is in the soul. If we have knowledge about it then breakthrough is guaranteed 100%. According, to **Hebrews 4:12-** we need to allow God to work in us to the level of dividing asunder of soul and spirit. The soul is an enemy of God and spirit and when we haven't managed to command it to obey the spirit, the results can be disastrous in prayer.

When we pass through situations that make us uneasy and uncomfortable, we feel that God has forsaken us. When we get to prayer with such emotions the soul gains control over our spirit. Note, that the devil can use our prayer to bring defeat to us. The soul pushes its own way and demands revenge; the soul desires to get even, the soul works something inside us that is against our spiritual prosperity.

Upon realization that while, we pray about something and thoughts concerning the same begin stemming out, instantly know that our prayers are influenced by the soul. Praying in the soul introduces trouble to the matter at hand.

As we wait upon God while in prayer, it's good to remember that: proper prayer changes things and the purpose of prayer is to obtain an answer. Prayer is work, discipline that brings desirable results. Prayer that connects with God gets an answer. Our responsibility is to provide an avenue where we can receive from God-Spirit man. Always, we need to yearn to bring the influence of God to the situations and problems at the time they occur. When we do so, the Holy Spirit speaks into our minds and it's at this point that the renewal of our minds is accomplished.

The Works of Patience

Let's look at **Isaiah 40:27-31**. Notice that patience is not merely a fixed determination to hold our place in the teeth of the wind, but to make actual progress in spite of it. Patience enables a person to move on determinedly. It may not be spectacular, but towards perfection. Patience will allow us to receive and participate in God's love as it builds loyalty and faithfulness as in the life of David. It will take us beyond our comfort zone into an area we don't want to go. Yet, when we do, we are better and more able to be used by God and to be available for others.

Patience will allow us to manage anger and problems, and to wait on God's timing. Consider the life of Hannah (**I Samuel 1:7**); after prayer, she went her way and began to eat. After praying and eating her face was no longer sad. Patience allows us to forgive, endure, and go on, even when we do not feel like it. It will see the hope that is ahead when the clouds of our lives and experiences block its view from our sight. It allows us to cling to Christ no matter what happens. Patience is that powerful attribute that enables a man and woman to remain steadfast under strain and continue pressing on. It's that quality that speaks out and says, "this too, will pass,…It's almost over…I can keep on." It brings out the knowledge that whatever happens, God is in control. Someday victory will be realized.

Patience is practiced…Whatsoever you want to be done unto you, do unto others.

Being patient to others does not mean we are weak, nor does it mean that we approve of their conduct. Though, we may hate their conduct and suffer keenly when it affects us, Christ tells us to bless them. This means we should offer favor upon them or give benefits to them. We can do this by wishing others well, speaking kindly of and to them, and seeking to do them good.

In combination with patience, the qualities of grace, mercy, loving kindness, goodness, love, joy, faithfulness, peace, gentleness, and self-control should be expressed. Just imagine, if God struck out at people just as short-tempered humans frequently do, no one would be alive today. Jonah, in a typically human reaction, wanted God to wipe the sinners of Nineveh, Israel's enemy, off the face of the earth (**Jonah 3:10**). II Peter 3:9 and Romans 2:3-6, show clearly that God's patience is exercised so; He can work on the situation to produce repentance.

Patience is showing tolerance unto others. It is accepting difficult situations from them, and God, without making demands or conditions. Patience allows us to endure a less than desirable situation. It allows us to put up with others who get on our nerves, without losing our characteristics of grace. Without patience, we cannot be effectively used in the lives of others, as they will appear abusive and unpleasant to us. *"He who is slow to wrath has great understanding, but he who is impulsive exalts folly."* (**Proverbs 14:29 NKJV**). "A wrathful man stirs up strife, but he who is slow to anger allays contention." (**Proverbs 15:18 NKJV**).

Patience is a virtue and we need to develop it in our lives. Patience is God's supernatural gift. Good interpersonal relationships depend on you doing your best, plus trusting God with the rest. We human beings are pitifully incomplete without God's Spirit. In Colossians 3: 12-13, Paul describes the nature of someone who's led by God's Spirit.

PRAYER

Lord, You alone know the depth of the burden we carry and You have measured the weight of it on our shoulders; but You are our refuge and strength, a very present help in trouble (Psalms 46:1). You have invited us to come boldly to the throne of grace, that we may obtain mercy and find grace to help in time of need. I come before Your throne and ask for grace to strengthen our hearts for any battle and give us patience to wait on You. Build us up, so that no matter what happens, we will be always rejoicing in hope, patient in tribulations, continuing steadfastly in prayer. Grant us endurance to run the race and not give up.

SUSY AMUSUGUT IKAPUYAN

Susy Amusugut Ikapuyan is a member of World Harvest Christian Centre in Nairobi, Kenya. She is a trained teacher who has taught in three different high schools since 2005. In her teaching experience and interaction with teenagers, the Lord has graced her to mentor, encourage, and help them locate their identity in society. She also serves the guidance and counseling department head in her current high school.

Susy joined World Harvest Christian Centre 2008. After fellowshipping for three years at World Harvest Christian Centre, she was heavily convicted that it was the Lord's doing and that she was under preparation for greater work in the ministry of the Lord, Jesus Christ. On August 22, 2010, she was appointed National Secretary of the women's ministry by the presiding Bishop Titus Imoite Papa and the First Lady Judith Imoite. In January 2011, she became the intercessory team leader On January 30, 2011, the Holy Spirit confirmed her as the teacher of the Word under Pastor David Osang'ir. Currently she is the coordinator and acting President of the Woman of God Ministries in Kenya.

Susy is married to Patrick Wanyonyi, another member of World

Harvest Christian Centre. They have three beautiful children: Vanessa, Grace, and David. Together, they serve the Lord because they believe that it is a blessing to serve the Lord.

CHAPTER 5

The Parable of an Answer to a Consistent and Effectual Prayer Life:

"A Prophetic Blueprint Revealed In the Ingredient Good"

Now, concerning the subject of the Fruit of the Spirit outlined in the scriptures as "good," or goodness and its role as it pertains to: "The 7 Ingredients To An Effective Prayer Life," I immediately began to enter into thought on the matter, and the Holy Spirit directed my thoughts toward the parable of the "good" Samaritan narrated by Jesus Christ in the scriptures. Let's take a look! In **Luke 10:25-37**, we can attest from the original context of the scripture that a certain "expert" in the law or lawyer stood up to challenge Jesus sought to provoke Him. Recognizing that Jesus was well educated and versed in the law and the prophets, he proposed a question to Jesus, by saying, "What shall I do to inherit eternal life?" Or prophetically speaking: "What shall I do to have or maintain a consistent and effectual prayer life?" Can you identify with this question? Are you in search of a more effectual and fervent relationship in prayer and communion with your heavenly Father? If so, as you journey with me through this chapter allow the Holy Spirit to minister to you.

As you follow along, you will see that not only was Jesus giving an example of the fruit of the Spirit (good/goodness); but was also imparting and divinely instituting a prophetic blueprint into the minds of those He taught. This prophetic nugget is a key component hidden inside of the fruit "good" that will take your relationship in prayer and all aspects of your Christian walk to another dimension. I would like to begin with a prayer.

Father, we acknowledge that you are the source of all knowledge and spiritual understanding. You are the originator of all life and purpose in the earth. You are worthy of all glory, honor, and praise. We forgive every person to the best of our understanding, of all trespasses and wrongful conduct we have received. We ask you Lord Jesus to forgive us of our attitudes, actions, and disobedience to your instructions in our lives. Wash and cleanse our minds today, so that we can receive your Word into "good" ground in our spirit man. Cleanse us from secret faults and presumptuous sins. Take us into your word and bless our understanding to grasp what we have learned. We pray this in Jesus name. Amen. Alright let us begin!

In Luke 10:25, the scripture opens with these words, "And, behold!" Let's stop there. There is purpose behind every single word that is written, proceeding out of the mouth of God. Every individual word or sentence structure should be deeply investigated to see what the Lord is saying and why. The word behold is defined in meaning as to observe, or regard with attention. So, let us take observation of what we are to behold in this scripture context. The scripture says, that a certain lawyer "stood up", and tempted Jesus referring to him as "Master". The attitude that God was targeting in this questionable display was that the lawyer stood up in a spirit of sarcasm. If you take the time to consider the action the lawyer demonstrated when he stood up, you will see that nonverbally; his body language exposed the pride of his inward condition that Jesus responded to in the next portion of this verse. You will also realize that this was not a simple person that stood up, but an educated lawyer; which challenged Jesus by his verbal salutation, Master, meaning teacher. Next, the lawyer presented Jesus with the question, "what must I" do to inherit eternal life?"

Jesus immediately saw the attitude and pride of this lawyer who personalized himself. Jesus also recognized the demon that wanted to tempt Him, using education in written law to find occasion and error in His demonstrations and message. Jesus saw in the lawyers' confidence that he was overly sure of his answer, so Jesus took the answer and opened it up to show the lawyer where he was spiritually lacking. (**Luke 10:28**). *"Be not deceived: evil communications corrupt good manners. Awake to righteousness and sin not: For some have not the knowledge of God: I speak this to your shame."* (**I Corinthians 15:33-34 KJV**).

Jesus' response to the lawyer was with a question referring to this very element! He said, *"What is written in the law?"* (**Luke 10:26 KJV**). In other words, what is your understanding of the scriptures since you are an expert in the law? The lawyer responded correctly according to what is written (**Deuteronomy 6:5**). Jesus acting as a good teacher or master praised his correct answer. He then caused the lawyer to see that though he knew the law, he had not put this commandment into practice according to his expertise. Jesus was attempting through the written word to free the lawyer of his flaw, with good inward works toward God and man (**Luke 10:27**). This would allot him, according to the promise of what was already written, eternal life in itself! Jesus began painting a picture of "Goodness", through the parable of the Good Samaritan. He reveals the inward mindset, which not only highlights this lawyers' effectiveness in his ability to make it to heaven, but good character and fruit by his works to present to God. Let's take a brief look at this text. Jesus speaks of a certain man who on his way down from Jerusalem to Jericho, fell among thieves, who stripped him of his clothes, wounded him, and left him for dead (**Luke 10:30-37**). Jesus was painting a picture to show that when the lawyer stood up, his pride, corrupted mannerisms, and lack of goodness in fruit of his character, fought against Jesus Christ.

Likewise, our conduct fights against the word. When we hear the truth at times, we strip the messenger who is speaking the truth with our dogma, or raised prideful attitude. We wound them with our defenses and walk off, leaving their words to fall dead on the ground, walking away as if we have done no harm. As pertaining to the body of Christ, entirely, there is a dilemma that is destroying and choking the "good fruit of the spirit" out of the body; which has now become commonly labeled "church hurt." This is the demon behind our actions and attitudes, that not only limits our ability to do good in accordance with what we preach, and how we religiously convene, but hinders our prayers from being effective. This delays the hand of God from moving swiftly to answer us (**Isaiah 59:1-7**). Looking back at our scripture passage, (**Luke 10:33**) we see the Priest, the Levite, and the Samaritan who all passed by the wounded man. The attitude of the Priest was as many of our responses today who hold a religious or spiritual office in the church world. When being challenged at the sight of a need we pass by and do not help. We are not walking in the good conduct of our understandings, as the lawyer also had not done, when faced with a real life situation.

We go on to observe the Levite, who also observed the wounded man. Gazing deeply at his condition, and probably wondering what happened, he looked at the man and passed on by to the other side. Just as we, who are more curious toward what constituted a calamity in someone's life and even ponder or discuss it, but have no intentions to actually administer healing to them. When we are not maintaining a consistent prayer life, we are not spiritually alert to demonstrate goodness though we claim to walk with God. Finally, the word spotlights the Samaritan. While he was journeying, he not only came to where the man was and observed him, but felt a sense of compassion for him. He went toward him and immediately began pouring oil and wine on his wounds. He then carried him to a place where he could have continual support and rest to recover mentally from his accident, completely compensated! The Samaritan did not stop or leave him without, but committed to the support of the man financially and physically, contributing to his well -being and ultimate success! We need to carefully examine our compassion and good intentions to graduate in our prayer lives. We should not only pray, but through much intercession and demonstration, portray this same example for mankind. God wants us to be detailed and fervent in our prayers and take good actions from this day forward!

My Personal Testimony

As I thought, meditated, and inquired of the Lord concerning this fruit of the Spirit, "Good" and its relationship to an effective prayer life, I was reminded of how the Holy Spirit opened my understanding prophetically through this scripture. I was able to shed light on my own experiences, as the scriptures unfolded one day. It was a correction and an admonishing at that time for me to examine this ingredient "good." I was able to measure my own actions physically, mentally, and emotionally regarding the souls that I passed-by and not assisted in my life's journey with the Lord. I had both been in the position of the man who was wounded, as well as those who passed him by. This is my testimony.

I remember when I first gave my heart to the Lord as a young man I had a great love for people. I desired to see people happy, support them, and do good toward them. I wanted the world to see Jesus in my life, as the song says, I wanted them to experience the goodness of the Lord I was determined to be the instrument that would demonstrate this to every person that I was around.

One day I had a conversation with the Holy Spirit concerning why I consistently had to be the one who demonstrated good to everyone, whether they responded the same or not. I constantly sacrificed my own thoughts, needs, and desire in order to maintain an effectual and close relationship with God. The Father responded to me saying, "I made you the way you are, and I made them the way they are." That was not the response I was looking for but what He said settled in my spirit and gave me peace. I knew then that it was my responsibility to walk unconditionally and be as the Lord had created me to be toward all men. Little did I know at the time, that this spiritual consistency was a prerequisite. It was a necessary component that would be a very strong foundation stone in my life, leading me to a very effective and effectual prayer life in God! As the years passed by, doing good continued, but the trials of life had catapulted to what seemed as more of a heavy burden. God's anointing upon my life pushed me toward perfecting the effectiveness of this fruit of the Spirit within me.

Twenty years later however, I saw that after experiencing a great deal of hardships, troubles, trials, losses, back to back crisis situations; and after overcoming those, I went on to greater challenges with demons. These were continuous and direct encounters with witchcraft, witches, and demonically delayed hindrances in high places. I came to the realization that my capacity for sympathy, compassion, and overall good fruits had severely decreased and plummeted to an all-time low. I began to notice that my spiritual wick was very short. My ability to feel compassion for my neighbor had waxed cold and diminished. I had become bitter and grumpy. I was the total flip side of an extremely compassionate and sympathetic person that would take the shirt off his own back and give it away on the spot. I was the person that would always give the best gifts. I would sacrifice my own bills and desired hobbies to help invest in another person's vision and work over my own because I loved to give. When I gave, I never looked back for a return.

Within twenty years, that person demonstrating the goodness of God became a picture in the many pages of my life. He was no longer a reality. Somewhere along the way I had lost taste for this fruit of the Spirit. I became disinterested in the needs of others. I slowly but surely found myself making excuses for why they were not worthy to receive my help, services, or even my prayers! Selfishness had begun to sprout its little head. I found myself praying for my own needs more than for others. I prayed for my own personal deliverances and slowly forgot how to care for others. I operated so long without my own needs being met and incurred many loses because this fruit of the spirit was no longer functioning within me in full measure. It went from full-time, to part-time, and then part-time to temporary and finally temporary to seasonal. I am not sharing this information from just from an intellectual standpoint but from my own life experiences. The Holy Spirit took me in deep observation to the same message in the Word of God, which I shared with you. I was delivered from a negative and bitter attitude, which stunted and delayed the accuracy and effectiveness of my prayers being assessed and answered!

God then challenged me. He helped me see that the same good, compassion, and care that I wanted someone. He even demonstrated for me what I needed to show people and He is my reward! An attitude cannot be cast out. It must be surgically dissected and properly dealt with in the Word of God, to produce salvation or change in that area. Today, I am not the same. Regardless of my tests, trials, and circumstances, I have gained compassion rather than losing it. I have become broken enough that the Holy Spirit can lead me and deal with me about others. Trials and tests, along with a balanced, detailed spiritual diet that consists of the right ingredients displayed in the Word of God will develop your effectiveness. It will do this not only in the fruit good but in all areas of your life and spiritual walk.

I am confident that by now the Holy Spirit, moving upon the Word of God has touched your heart and understanding to operate in the fruit of goodness and care as you walk with the Lord.

The keys inside of this parable of the Good Samaritan reveal to us our blueprint for a powerfully effective prayer life. The word of God is fully packed with these treasures. But as the Word says, how can one hear without a preacher and how can one preach unless he is sent! God bless you.

APOSTLE ZARIE M. THOMAS

Pastor/Apostle Zaire M. Thomas along with Elect Lady Prophetess Marybeth Thomas (Power of a Nazarite Ministries) founded Gospel of Christ Crusades (GOCC). GOCC started as a subsidiary ministry birthed out of its headquarters, True Foundation World Outreach Ministries, Inc. Topeka, KS. Under the direction and "Great Commission" of the Holy Spirit, GOCC has become the "Spear-Head" and focus that has propelled this ministry into worldwide evangelism. GOCC is designed to rescue souls revive the perishing, and equip and position the nations of the world for the "Greatest Revival" on earth before the coming of our Savior Jesus Christ (Isaiah 61).

Pastor/Apostle Zaire M. Thomas is also the author of "Wisdom's Cry: A Prophetic, Deeper Level" publication brought forth for a generation that desires to dig up and seek out the "wells" of the ancient "old paths." Through the Prophetic Word of God, preached and taught from the anointing of God upon his life, Apostle Thomas is known as one who can reach any age and any generation. The wisdom, balance, and skill God has placed upon Apostle Zaire Thomas from the same instructed, proven, and manifested Word of

God that our forefathers in the word treaded and replenished has brought many men and women of God to great success in their spiritual lives by the simple truth of the gospel (Jeremiah 6:16-17)! To be a recipient of the life and ministry of Apostle Zaire Thomas, please do not hesitate to correspond for engagements or spiritual edification. May the God of peace take you to new dimensions in your spiritual life.

CHAPTER 6

Maintaing "Faithfulness" A "Prepared" Package

The bible speaks about a fruit of the Spirit, "faith." More than standing at the door of desire for this fruit, it becomes our responsibility to find out how to lay hold upon it, partake, and process it in order to go to the next step, faithfulness. Many of us are not taught to how to seek God. Therefore, we remain incompetent in such an intricate area as faith. This cripples our ability to acquire faithfulness and our lives reflect it. We are strengthened in our measure of faith and then we lose sight somewhere along the way. We are not consistent so there is no change to this cycle. I am confident that after reading this chapter, not only will you lay hold upon faith but also, each reader will experience a change in the degree of understanding God's Word, which produces, sustains, and brings forth fruits of faithfulness. Using the word as our guide and the Holy Ghost as our instructor, let us receive the engrafted word of truth upon the pages of our hearts and be renewed in the spirit of our mind! We shall acquire a direct focus, "maintaining faithfulness" in an effectual prayer life.

Now, that the focus is set, there are two aspects of thought to consider; so that we study in the right direction. 1) How do we develop in our faith? 2) How do we maintain faithfulness in an effectual prayer life? It is very important to realize that the greatest source of hearing the voice of God speak to us after we pray is not limited to accessing the spirit realm or to a word in the mouth of a messenger of God alone. It is by referring to what God has already written and prepared in the holy bible. Studying the Word of God after prayer is key to a balanced communicative relationship with God.

Developing in Our Faith

Getting back to the basics of a Christian walk is the first step to developing in our faith. Many of us place more value or emphasis upon using our faith for new heights and dimensions in God. In reality we have left or are yet unstable in the foundations of Christian walk. We develop faithfulness continuously obeying the Word of God after we pray. The great men and women of the bible were used as living physical examples that walking with God, maintaining a consistent prayer life, and obeying His word by faith, works! A faithful disciple of Christ should not strive to sharpen prophetic gifts or abilities in spiritual concepts immediately after they learn that that they have a great purpose in Christ. **I Peter 2:2** states: that as a newborn babe, one should desire the sincere milk of the word in order that they may grow thereby. A spiritual dysfunction develops when sheep have no shepherd who tend to them in daily guidance, or counsel, and are not involved in their personal decisions in life. Additionally, when sheep are exposed to knowledge outside of their shepherd, fall behind in following their shepherd, or rebel while receiving assistance from their shepherd, their demonstration, and conduct lacks in pinpointing where they are planted and rooted. This is why there are so many spirit-filled Christians who are tormented, oppressed, stressed, and defeated by demons that take advantage of their independence.

Operations of the five- fold ministry (apostle, prophet, pastor, evangelist, and teacher) within this type of believer become limited as to how far into the planting of the Lord they in turn can bring God's people. **Psalms 1:1-5**, teaches us that walking outside of the protection and counsel of pastorship, and not being planted properly, leads mankind not only to self -destruction within our own lives, but we hinder the absolute salvation of others and thus fade away. When we are properly planted in good soil under good leadership, we learn to understand that circumstances of life. This builds the stability that faith empowers and keeps us near the cross that we may be properly nourished, tutored, and refreshed in God's presence. Outside of this as a vessel of the Lord, we operate in spiritual demonstrations but remain damaged and even polluted on the inside of our person. On the other hand, there is such a need for shepherds after God's own heart that God has predestined to feed the flock according to scripture. The bible says, that faith comes by hearing, and hearing by the Word of God, taught by those who God actually sends to preach the word to those who have an ear to hear it! What we have learned so far has already catapulted our faith to a better quality of believing;

by understanding where we need to place ourselves. We also have acquired the balance, which spiritual assistance produces, to grow properly from this point. Let us now hear what the Spirit of God has to say to us, as we go on to the next phase of this chapter; maintaining faithfulness.

Maintaining Faithfulness in an Effectual Prayer Life

It is important to realize that faith is experiencing substantiality beyond natural mental and physical capacity. It is powerfully bestowed upon our lives when we hear the Word of God preached being mixed with faith. There is the divine nature of God, (fruits of the spirit) which supersedes standard religiosity, human knowledge, and earthly, natural, age-born experiences. It is the key to inheriting the blessing of faithfulness consistently. The fruits of the Spirit of God are all results of a predetermined, predestined, perceived, and a prepared package sent by God to us. It is sent to those who believe and are ready to not only accept salvation through Jesus Christ, but the things He has prepared for us who continue in Him. As we go along through this last segment of chapter, it will be beneficial for you to follow each scripture referenced; so that you can see all that the Spirit of God reveals within His word with the writings of this chapter. Many times, it is our own understanding that diverts truth, and causes us to miss the point that the Spirit of God is trying to convey to our lives.

"And he shewed me a pure river of water of life, clear as crystal, proceeding out of the throne of God and of the Lamb. In the midst of the street of it, and on either side of the river, was there the tree of life, which bare twelve manner of fruits, and yielded her fruit

every month: and the leaves of the tree were for the healing of the nations. And there shall be no more curse: but the throne of God and of the Lamb shall be in it; and his servants shall serve him: And they shall see his face; and his name shall be in their foreheads. And there shall be no night there;...and they shall reign for ever and ever. And he said unto me, these sayings are 'faithful' and true." (**Revelation 22:1-6 KJV**).

In order, for our faith to contain what God wants us to see, we must carefully take time to examine this scripture. Maintaining faithfulness is now operating within us and shall become a disciplined attribute as we develop consistency in digesting God's Word. The more we study the word of God, the more we retain it.

Let us explore **Revelation 22:1**, the word shewed (showed) means to escort, usher, guide, or assist. The word assists means to give aid. We can clearly say that the Holy Spirit of God has escorted, ushered, or is guiding us directly; in this passage to a pure river of water of life in the spirit. The Holy Spirit shall assist us with the revelation of His message within the scripture. The physical description "clear as crystal," displays a very important spiritual essence. The word clear means pure, free from darkness or obscurity, full of light, which is (understanding). Crystal is described as a highly transparent or brilliant type of glass. We now have gained the understanding that this river of water of life. Its description and source represents the reflection the Word of God carries in being open for all to see clearly, as well as bringing clarity and pureness to our understandings and lives. If we faithfully, visit and examine, the word of God afterward praying and meditating daily upon it, we should always have a tremendous life changing experience in our spiritual, mental, and physical livelihood. There is a prophetic content that God wanted us to understand and transition into as we become faithful in searching.

Let us continue exploring **Revelation 22**, this passage states: that on either side of the river and in the midst of it was there the tree of life, yielding twelve manner of fruit every month, in its season. If you can travel back in the Word of God, with me, the description in this passage is similar to the Garden of Eden, described in **Genesis 2:15-17**. Although scientists and archeologists are trying to still locate this physical site, God hid "the way" of it. He placed an angel to stand guard over that "way" with a sword drawn to prevent any passage; preserving mankind from living in an eternal spiritual corruption (knowing good and evil **Genesis 3:24**). According to our text, (**Revelation 22:1-2**) this way is now made open through Jesus Christ. Maintaining an unbreakable relationship with God in a faithful and effective prayer life is now possible! As you see, next in Revelation 22:3, this everlasting corrupted state of being, was a CURSE; that has been broken! As a result of this powerful redemption, when we visit the throne of God, in prayer; we should not leave without an answer from the Lord. God wants more than our religious rituals and faithful tithing. God wants to take us in the spirit within His word through dimensions of prayer where our limited devotions, ignorance, partial teachings, and lack of faith have prevented. Today, we are experiencing a walk with God through His word, producing effectiveness when we pray. We must go back to the word now.

It is important when we pray to always have a bible handy, so that God can speak to us, through what is already prepared and written there. Remember, we don't have to strain for a word from

God, or seek a prophecy. God has already supplied all of the words we need to carry us through life's journey in 66 books of the Holy Bible. Take a moment and read **Genesis 3:3-5**. If you notice, God reveals an answer to the mystery of the "way" Eve became deceived. This was not the "way" of the Lord. This was another way devised by Satan to destroy her relationship with God. Notice, the question Satan presented to Eve. *"Yea, has God said ye shall not....."* (**Genesis 3:4 KJV**).

In order for Satan to deceive Eve with words into breaking God's commandment, he had to speak in like manner (like God), to get her attention, thus "yea." He then referenced what was already spoken by proposing the statement in a question form causing Eve to answer. Confusion took place and Eve's curiosity was activated. Watch the tricks of Satan as you follow Christ. Allow your shepherd to guide you. Remember, God's sheep know His voice and will not follow a Satan tempted Eve to experience an area of the garden that was not yet to be touched, without a guide, or usher!

Due to Satan's attempt to hurt God and destroy man, he broke rank and prompted Eve's thoughts and attention directly to the area of his interest; the tree of the knowledge of good and evil. Sin developed in Eve. After taking of the fruit, she spread the same disobedient advice to Adam as he ate, sinning as well. A disturbance at that point occurred and a faithful commitment shattered. This disturbance and broken commitment, not only affected the relationship between God and man, but total dependency man had upon God. This dependency was the ability to properly follow and obey the guide and leading of the Lord. Disobedience and all manner of fruitful sinful nature has disturbed the human race ever since. Consider the state of humanity today. We operate in same trap of confusion, curiosity, and act of disobedience, Satan uses when he distracts us. This causes us to rationalize with God's original truth and leads us astray in our independent nature. We are tempted and tested as a result we fail in faithfulness. If you notice, the very moment that sin takes place we pull away from prayer. It was a curse within our flesh to keep failing in our spiritual walk. Jesus said within this river of water of life there would be no more curse (**Revelation 22:3**)! He promised that His word would be faithful and true. We would become his servants and reign for ever more (**Revelation 22:3-6**)! The Blood of Jesus has cleansed all of heaven, the earth, the garden, and the entire human race forever.

So, why are we still walking in disobedience? Because we are not aware that we are been purified by this river and can come back into the proper "way" of God's divine order. All, we have to do now is follow our guide. The Holy Spirit, today, has indeed led us back to God. We are led back to basics in our faith, back to sound teaching, and to a bountiful faithful river of water of life; which we can experience in prayer flowing continually in our direction. This river of water of life will sustain every man who drinks from it for eternity. Now, that you have this insight, you will never be the same again. Ask God for his help.

Pray this prayer: *Father, I thank You that no matter where I am spiritually, in the belly of hell or the highest form of heaven, You can find me. Today, I have learned that it is okay to need You. Help me to find a good church and place myself under good counsel and tutorship. I will be humble enough to depend on You Lord. I thank You for this in Jesus name. Amen.* Now, continue to seek God, obey Him, and watch Him take you to places you would not have realized. His word is already prepared, packaged, and delivered to you through His shepherd, Jesus Christ!

PROPHETESS MARYBETH THOMAS

Prophetess MaryBeth Thomas (Power of a Nazarite Ministries), along with Pastor/Apostle Zaire M. Thomas founded Gospel of Christ Crusades (GOCC). GOCC started as a subsidiary ministry birthed out of its headquarters, True Foundation World Outreach TFWO) Ministries, Inc. Topeka, KS. Under the direction and "Great Commission" of the Holy Spirit, GOCC has become the "Spear-Head" and focus that has propelled this ministry into worldwide evangelism. GOCC is designed to rescue souls revive the perishing, and equip and position the nations of the world for the "Greatest Revival" on earth before the coming of our Savior Jesus Christ (Isaiah 61).

Power of a Nazarite Ministries, Founder Prophetess MaryBeth Thomas, serves as a strong wall of intercession and spiritual warfare, to go before and follow behind the great work of Apostleship TFWO Ministries carry. Power of a Nazarite Ministries has even gone into the personal lives and homes of many around the world, causing them to rise from depression, oppression, and faithlessness in prayer. Leading them to obtaining promises and seeing answers from God, as well as, teaching and instructing men and women how to walk in the faith of God's miracle working power, and how to live a consecrated and devoted lifestyle that accompanies these results. For more information, or to request a conference or meeting at your location, please feel free to correspond. May the God of peace continue to address and bless your heart, Amen!

CHAPTER 7

The Fruits of the Spirit - Humbleness and Self-Control

"A True and Faithful Servant"

Many times God will speak a message into your spirit giving specific revelation and direction for your life. I thought I had a great knowledge on that word, but since I decided to write about my walk with the Father regarding humbleness and self- control it has been an experience.

Humbleness is having a spirit of humility, meekness and carrying a servant heart. It's also a state of mind well pleasing with God. It preserves the tranquility and makes us patience when under trials. When it comes to being humble, we must be willing to sacrifice, love and lay down our lives for others, so the Christ like humility can come forth, and set others free from bondage. Jesus is our perfect example of understanding and experience of being humble until death. He never boasted about how He walked in humbleness. We must remember that He gave up His life, so we have ever-lasting life. *"5Let this same attitude and purpose and (humble) mind be in you which was in Christ Jesus (Let Him be your example in humility). 6Who, although being essentially one with God and in the form of God (possessing the fullness of the attributes which make God God), did not think this equality with God was a thing to be eagerly grasped or retained. 7But stripped Himself (of all privileges and rightful dignity), so as to assume the guise of a servant (slave), in that He became like men and was born a human being. 8And after He had appeared in human form, He abased and humbled Himself (still further) and carried His obedience to the extreme of death, even the death of the cross."* (**Philippians 2:5-8 Amplified Bible AMP**). What makes us think we shouldn't do as Jesus? He died on the cross for all mankind. He never once backed away or said God I don't want to do this for them.

In the book of Matthews 26: 36-46, it speaks of how God was with Peter and two sons of Zebedee at Gethsemane knowing that He would be betrayed by one of his Disciples. Every time He went away and prayed the first time saying, *"O Father if it possible let this cup pass from me nevertheless not as I will, but as thou wilt."* (**Matthew 26:39 KJV**). Jesus said this each time He went away to pray to the Father, in fact He went away three times to the Father saying *"O Father if this cup may not pass away from me, except I drink it, thy will be done."* (**Matthew 26:42 KJV**). This was a question to me as God was sharing with me about His son. So many times, we have situations and unanswered prayers during our walk with the Father. He gracefully reminds us each day that our walk has nothing to do with us but for others to see the Christ in us. We come to the Father with little faith, not believing in His promises for others and us. We read, talk, and perform plays about what Jesus did on the Cross. If you were faced with what Jesus did for us, what would you do? The word of God says, *"God so loved the world he gave his only begotten Son. That whosoever believeth in him should not perish but have everlasting life."* (**John 3:16 KJV**) That's an awesome sacrifice!

Looking into the word of God throughout the Bible, we see that Jesus would never rush into anything without getting before the Father. Even when Jesus was tempted, the first thing He would do is go away to be with the Father and pray. Now don't take it wrong, Jesus knew what His purpose was on earth. He knew he would lay down His life for us. Jesus never complained, nor did He stop praying. He just continued to do what His purpose was on the earth.

It is hard to wait on God to answer sometimes when circumstances and chaos is surrounding us. We want Him to answer us now right now. *"But they that wait upon the Lord shall renew (their) strength; they shall mount up with wings as eagles; they shall run, and not be weary; (and) they shall walk, and not faint."* (**Isaiah 40:31 KJV**). It's telling us that we should never second-guess God in our circumstance. It shows that we must be willing to pray and wait on God.

The word humbleness comes from humility. It was exhibited in Jesus' walk on the earth. It also carries a servant heart as Jesus served us. A Servant is one who's willing to sacrifice, love, and lay down their lives. Be an example as a servant. *"This is a faithful saying and worthy of all acceptation. For therefore we both labor and suffer reproach, because we trust in the living God, who is the Savior of all men, especially of those that believe. These things command and* teach. *Let no man despise thy youth; but be thou an example of the believers, in word, in conversation, in charity, in spirit, in faith in purity."* (**I Timothy 4:9-12 KJV**). A true servant has patience, doesn't complain and they will endure until the end. This is what Jesus did for us on the cross, not once did we hear Him complain. Not once did He respond back to the people while on the cross. His words were:

"Then said Jesus, Father forgive them; for they know not what they do. And they parted his raiment and cast lots." (**Luke 23:34 KJV**).

What would you have done? I know for me I would have said, "Really God you want me to die for them?" See Jesus wanted what God wanted for us, so He was willing to lay down His life for us. Jesus even interceded for us at his final hours. John 17: 1- *"These words spake Jesus and lifted up his eyes to heaven and said Father, the hour is come glorify thy Son, that thy Son also may glorify. As thou hast given him power over flesh, that he should give eternal life to as many as thou has given him. And this is life eternal, that they might know thee the only true God, and Jesus Christ whom thou hast sent. I have glorified thee on the on the earth; I have finished the work which thou gavest me to do."* (**John 17:1-4**). Looking over Jesus life, He was such a lovely, long-suffering, and patient person. He wanted the best for us. He wasn't concerned about the cost. He loved us so much that He laid down His life. This is why we should be shouting for joy and willing to do everything that the Father instructs us to do. I can feel the hot fire of the Holy Spirit moving in me as I think about what Jesus did for me. How could anyone continue not to love and serve the God that gave His only son? It takes the Holy

Spirit dwelling in us daily and having self-control over our lives to understand what Jesus did for us on the cross. That's where self-control comes into play.

Self-control in the biblical term is temperance. It means inward strength and restraint. Self-control is the inward strength to bring all physical appetites under the control of the Holy Spirit. Humbleness and self-control impact our destiny. *"A man without self-control is like a city broken into and left without walls."* (**Proverbs 25:28 ESV**). *"For this very reason, adding your diligence (to the divine promises), employ every effort in exercising your faith to develop virtue (excellence, resolution, Christian energy), in an (exercising) virtue (develop) knowledge (intelligence), And in (exercising) knowledge (develop) self-control and in (exercising) steadfastness (develop) godliness (piety). And in (exercising) godliness (develop) brotherly affection, and in (exercising) brotherly affection (develop) Christian love."* (**II Peter 1:5-7 AMP**). It is walking in obedience to the leading of God's Spirit that produce humbleness and self-control, because that is the work of the Holy Spirit which Jesus left us, the Comforter.

Self-control has a way of escape for us. *"No temptation has overtaken you that is not common to man. God is faithful, and he will not let you be tempted beyond your ability, but with the temptation he will also provide the way of escape, that you may be able to endure it."* (**I Corinthians 10:13 ESV**). God is good. What person, love one, children, parents, or employer would provide that for you when situations and temptations comes your way and do that for you? God has a way of escape, but you must have a personal relationship with Him. Place your faith and trust in God promises. God has made this available to all. *"For the grace of God has appeared, bringing salvation for all people, training us to renounce ungodliness and worldly passions, and to live self-controlled, upright, and godly lives in the present age, waiting for our blessed hope, the appearing of the glory of our great God and Savior Jesus Christ, who gave himself for us to redeem us from all lawlessness and to purity for himself a people for his own possession who are zealous for good works."* (**Titus 2:11-14 ESV**).

Humbleness and self-control are the same in one way that when you are humble you are not putting yourselves first, caring about your only needs and wants or uncaring of other. You are ready to be a true servant to others and have self-control or shall we say have temperance meaning inward strength (the Holy Spirit) to control our appetites and our mouth. Our mouth always seems to get us into trouble, meaning out of the will of God. We must learn to accept peacefully, yield, and work our way through with fasting and praying.

There is no one thing you can speak about without knowing that everything can be resolved by praying for self-control and displaying humbleness. Remember God is always in control, we just fail to yield to His voice. We as born-again believers find ourselves sometime not being humble and out of control when situations or people don't respond the way we want. We believe that we have the right to act the way we do sometimes out of the nature of God.

God want us to understand that humbleness is not when we are weak. It's when we hear the voice of God instructing us to move in meekness. *"Love suffer long and is kind; love does not envy; love does not parade itself, is not puffed up."* (**I Corinthians 13:4 NKJV**). This is how Jesus flowed while on the earth, by the Holy Spirit. My favorite verse is **I Corinthians 9:19-23**.

"For though I am free from all men, I have made myself a servant to all, that I might win the more; and to the Jews I became as a Jew, that I might win Jews; to those who are under the law, as under the law that I might win those who are without law, to the weak I became weak, that I might win the weak. I have become all things to all men that I might by all means save some. Now this I do for the gospel's sake, that I may be partaker of it with you." (**I Corinthians 9:19-23 NKJV**). I want to leave you with this prayer in closing.

Father, I want to repent for the way that I responded today. I know that You're my Daddy that forgives me when I'm out of line so I thank You. Your loving kindness, peace, and joy to me are everything. I can't live without it. I know You laugh and smile at me when I don't listen but Your patience toward me is awesome, again thank You so much. You're revealing Yourselves to me in Your word and in my quiet time of prayer daily. I want to be a true servant to Your people, so they can see Christ in me. It's my desire that my life points them back to You. Father, You deserved all the glory in my life. I send all my praises to You because You're worthy of all my praises. Continue to reveal in me what is not like You. I have faith and I trust you that I'm going to walk toward You each day I pray. Father, it is my desire to be well- pleasing unto You in Jesus Name, Amen.

PASTOR ANGELA BRADLEY

Angela Bradley is pastor and prophet of The Plan Ministries, under the leadership of Apostle Carnal Bradley, her loving husband and Founder/Overseer of the ministry.

Angela has a tremendous passion for God's Word coupled with a love for God's people. She has a contagious spirit of generosity that flows through every facet of her ministry. Pastor Angela often says, "I just want to do what God wants me to do and always be in the right position to hear His (God) voice." That's her motto. Her vision is uncompromisingly clear, with one central principle; to build and develop a Kingdom of empowered people for the Kingdom of God that they may establish a pure and personal relationship with God.

Pastor Angela knows that praying always without ceasing and proclaiming the word of God in every situation is what God is calling His people to do at this time. God has instructed and anointed her to continue to pray, so that the movement and a repositioning takes place, for the work that is before us shall be accomplished. Pastor Angela is an effective vessel used by God to help restore the Kingdom of God. It is her heart's desire to see bondage broken off God's people, and to see them come into the "Oneness" of God. Whatever the Father says to her, you can guarantee that she will do it without compromising or watering down God's Word. She will speak the pure truth.

Pastor Angela has been serving God's people for over forty years, but most remember her as an awesome servant to God's people. She is one of the authors for the Daughters of Distinction book entitled "Seven Ingredients to an Effective Pray Life (Volumes 3-5)."

She has two wonderful children Vincent and Tonoah and six grandchildren whom she loves dearly.

TABLE OF CONTENTS

VOLUME VII HONESTY

Keeping it Real in Prayer	73
God Honors Honesty	84
Press Toward Honesty	93
Alone in a Room	102
Honesty	110
The Spirit of Truth	120
Possessing the Integrity of Joseph	129

CHAPTER 1

Keeping it Real in Prayer

When can real healing and deliverance take place? Upon entering any recovery program, the first step is admitting the problem. Another step involves taking ownership. The same can be applied in holiness. God cannot truly help if we are not honest with him and admit our weaknesses and struggles. It is time to be real with God in prayer. Included within this chapter are several obstacles which inhibit an honest relationship with Jesus. Allow this chapter to serve as a guide through a self-analysis in your personal prayer life.

Shed the Persona

Not surprisingly, people hold many titles, carry several positions, and in the process put on many masks. The definition of persona refers to the masks once used to convey certain characters in a dramatic production. Likewise, from that definition it is apparent that a persona is not the true person but rather a character portrayal. Merriam-Webster (2013) gives several definitions as follows "**a** plural personas: an individual's social facade or front that especially in the analytic psychology of C. G. Jung reflects the role in life the individual is playing —**b** : the personality that a person (as an actor or politician) projects in public." Thus, in reality people present themselves in a light that is not entirely accurate. According to Genesis 3:7, when Adam and Eve knew they were naked, the first thing they did was find fig leaves in attempt to cover up. Then they hid from God. Evidently, since the fall of man, people have attempted to cover up when God designed for us to come naked before Him. We laugh to cover pain. We present ourselves as overly confident to cover insecurity. We tell lies to hide the truth. We wear fancy clothes, drive expensive cars, and live in big houses. Meanwhile, our souls are desolate. We are drowning in despair. God is not impressed by the outward appearance. He looks at the heart (**1 Samuel 16:7**).

Sometimes it is necessary to shield inner hurt to function. However, when we come before God in prayer it is time to come naked. We must remove every falsehood because He sees and knows all. In some instances, I recall praying in a manner in which I avoided mentioning my deepest hurt because I wanted to show God that I was grown up or mature. I was tired of crying over the same issues. I felt I was wasting His time. On the contrary, Jesus experienced our pain. He bridged the gap so that we can openly come to Him. *"For we do not have a high priest who is unable to empathize with our weaknesses, but we have one who has been tempted in every way, just as we are--yet he did not sin"* (**Hebrews 4:15 NIV**). Therefore, I encourage you to enter boldly into the throne room of grace and place your petitions before Jesus (**Hebrews 4:16**). In the quest to be real with God, remove the masks. Shed the persona(s), live as the fearfully and wonderfully made individual God created, and allow Jesus to heal your heart.

Come Clean

Sometimes in prayer, we fervently attempt to tear down strongholds over others while neglecting to address personal hidden sins deterring the move of God. According to **I John 1:8**, if we think we have not sinned, we deceive ourselves. A common misconception among believers is the "once saved, always saved" mentality. My friends, this is not biblical. In fact, believers can very well fall back into sin. We know that the unrighteous will not inherit the kingdom. However, some believers willfully practice sin and think because they are saved they will make it to heaven. Additionally, 1 Corinthians 6:9 tells us those practicing the following sins will not enter the kingdom: fornication, idolatry, adultery, homosexuality, sexual perversion, robbery, coveting, drunkenness, abusing others, and extortion. Furthermore, there are hidden sins in which we often overlook because they are masked as habits or as personal characteristics such as lying, backbiting, gossip, stubbornness, unbelief, arrogance, disobedience, unsubmissiveness, murmuring, cursing, and so forth. Even if you perform sin in secret, God sees, and knows. The fact is that a tree is known by its fruit. Thus, actions are demonstrative of the type of tree you are. *"I the Lord search the heart, I try the reins, even to give every man according to his ways, and according to the fruit of his doings."* (**Jeremiah 17:10 KVJ**).

Furthermore, God only holds us accountable to our knowledge; hence the reason Adam and Eve originally were naked and uncorrupted. Whenever, God gives a commandment, and that command is broken, the consequence is judgment. In a sense, ignorance can serve as a safety net. However, as God reveals His truth and as we mature in Christ, we are held accountable. *"Therefore to him that knoweth to do good, and doeth it not, to him it is sin."* **(James 4:17 KJV)**.

Understandably, there is a difference between battling the sin nature of man and willfully sinning. Once we have accepted Jesus, the devil undoubtedly will test in those areas where there was weakness. However, *"there hath no temptation taken you but such as is common to man: but God is faithful, who will not suffer you to be tempted above that ye are able; but will with the temptation also make a way to escape, that ye may be able to bear it."* (**I Corinthians 10:13 KJV**).

Friends, I encourage you today to ask God to show you the hidden sins in your heart and be willing to accept that you have sinned. Whereas, Christians are no longer regarded as unbelievers, our lifestyles must reflect change. God is not in the condemning business. Rather He chastises those who He loves (**Hebrews 12:6**). Today, our father is letting us know we are missing the mark, and it is time to get back on track.

Stop Being Selfish

In actuality, many are guilty of seeking God's hand and not His face. Our prayers are laced with desires that contradict God's will. In fact, we can neglect to even ask God's will. Thus, our prayers consist of Lord; I need a new car, house, husband, wife, and so forth. **James 4:2-3 (KJV)** states: *"Ye lust, and have not: ye kill, and desire to have, and cannot obtain: ye fight and war, yet ye have not, because* *ye ask not, Ye ask, and receive not, because ye ask amiss, that ye may consume it upon your lusts."* Desires become lustful when the motive for asking is wrong. Why do you want that bigger house? What is the reason for that new car? Are you lusting after someone else's spouse or coveting your neighbor's lifestyle? The fact is God already knows what we need (**Matthew 6:8**). Furthermore, God's will is that provisions are met. However, He instructs us to seek His kingdom first (**Matthew 6:33**). Thus, our focus in prayer should not primarily be about tangible items, rather about the work of the Kingdom. According to **Psalm 37:4**, if you take delight in serving the Lord, he will give what your heart desires.

Until, we can submit fully to God's will; the devil will continue to be right at the doorstep of our souls looking for an opportunity to come back in through our soulish realm and inserting an insatiable hunger that will not be quenched. Stormie Omartian said it best, "Don't keep telling God what you want without asking him what He wants" (p. 59).

Examine your love walk with Jesus today. If you only pray when you want something, you are only looking for the fishes and loaves (John 6:26). Though it may seem some of your prayers will be answered, your relationship and prayer life with Jesus is limited. Furthermore, you will not fully understand the miracles that He performs every day. "When your spirit is centered on God, all activities he initiates will be noble, full of peace, natural, and so spontaneous that it will appear to you there has hardly been any activity at all" (p. 102).

Be Free From Religion

Often, I am asked what is my religious preference and in response

I kindly state I have a relationship with Jesus Christ; I am a Christian. As Christians, it is important to differentiate between a religious connotation and a true relationship with our Savior. Not surprisingly, the difference is apparent in assessing one's prayer language and the context thereof. In **Matthew (6:6-7)**, Jesus instructed the disciples to pray in secret and not to pray using vain repetitions as unbelievers do. Jesus desires intimacy with us. Anyone who is married understands that intimacy requires time spent. However, to truly become one with your spouse the typical location is behind closed doors. Likewise, Jesus desires that we not only profess Him in public as many do; rather your alone time with Him reflects the passion and deep commitment you have with Him.

In observation of other religions, salvation is presumed attainable through works. Thus, certain hours of servitude are required; particular garments are worn on certain occasions; followers enter the place of worship at set times and dates and so forth. Unfortunately as Christians, many have fallen into similar religious traps such as certain practices, rituals, traditions, and attire by which we classify ourselves as Christians. This is not God's will. As mentioned in **Matthew 27:51**, the veil has been torn. Thus, we can enter into the holy of holies boldly, meaning we have regular access to our Savior through prayer. "Don't become attached to any form of formal prayer, not matter how good it may appear. It is no longer good for you if it turns you aside from what God desires of you" (p. 92).

Take a moment to examine the content of your prayers. Do you find yourself repeating phrases, trying to sound educated, praying only at church, praying loudly so that others hear you, being puffed up and self-righteous, and condemning others. Additionally, assess your reason for being a Christian: is it out of obligation, ritual, or habit? If this is the case, repent of that religious spirit and ask the Holy Spirit to make intercession so that you can pray accordingly (**Romans 8:26**).

Be Specific

Previously, in my prayer life, I would not tell God what I needed. As mentioned, God knows what we need (**Matthew 6:8**). Therefore, I would neglect to tell Him. However, I failed to realize that by not telling Jesus what I needed, I was creating a barrier in our relationship. Jesus desires open communication with us. He considers us friends, yet, we are also His children. Not surprisingly, you may be thinking; "Hold on. You told me not to ask God for stuff." Please understand relationship involves two-way communication. As mentioned, we should not only go to God with self-centered, lust inspired desires. Rather we should listen for His voice and direction. We should ask Him what He needs from us. Jeanne Guyon mentioned throughout her book *Experiencing God Through Prayer*, the importance of silence in prayer. Likewise, Guyon mentions the significance of releasing our concerns to Jesus. In other words, when your heart is turned toward the Lord, your desires are no longer for a selfish purpose. According to I John 3:22, when you keep His commandments and do what is pleasing before God, you can ask and receive from the Lord. Thus, the motive behind your desires transforms. Consequently, the prayer is, "Lord, I need a new car so that I can drive people to church" or "Lord I want to be a blessing to the kingdom financially."

A few years ago, I recall hearing the voice of the Holy Spirit one night as I slept. He said, "Renatta, ask of me." In another instance,

He said "Renatta, command of me." I arose out of my sleep and immediately went to the Bible. I was unaware that we could command of the Lord. I thought that would be disrespectful. However, **Isaiah 45:11 (KVJ)** states: *"Thus saith the LORD, the Holy One of Israel, and his Maker, Ask me of things to come concerning my sons, and concerning the work of my hands command ye me."* In other words, we can tell God exactly what we need in our lives. Furthermore, **Matthew 18:18** says, that whatever we bind on earth shall be bound in heaven, and whatever we lose on earth shall be loosed in heaven. God is telling us we have relationship as His children. Therefore, because of that relationship when we make our requests, those requests will reflect His Word and will. The fact is we cannot ask amiss if we are truly in Christ, and make our requests according to the promises of God. *"If ye abide in me, and my words abide in you, ye shall ask what ye will, and it shall be done unto you"* (**John 15:7 KJV**).

My friends in Christ, ask yourselves today, what you have attempted to hold on to? What matters do you avoid when in prayer to your Heavenly Father? He desires your truth. He desires your vulnerability. Give Him all your cares, for he cares for you (**I Peter 5:7**).

Conclusion: The Reality Check

Throughout this chapter, I pray you have taken the time to assess your prayer life. It is time to be real, admit weaknesses and take responsibility. The good news is that there is hope. God has so graciously provided opportunity for redemption and restoration. Please pray the following prayer.

Seven Ingredients To An Effective Prayer Life

Dear Lord, I love you and I return to you. Teach me how to pray. I desire your Holy Spirit to dwell within me to intercede. I am battling _____. I am aware that I have to fully admit my issues to receive true deliverance. I acknowledge the sin in my life and repent. I acknowledge that at times I attempt to hide my true self from you. I am guilty of a religious spirit, but I desire relationship with you. Lord, I submit myself to you. I pray that your will be done in my life. Remove the selfish and lustful desires. Thank you Jesus for the opportunity to come before you this day. In Jesus' name, Amen.

EVANGELIST RENATTA JONES

Evangelist Renatta Jones was born and raised in Pontiac, Michigan. At the age of seven, she was baptized in Jesus' name. In that same year, she was filled with the Holy Spirit. Evangelist Jones currently holds a Master's and Bachelors of Science in Psychology and an Associates of Arts in Business from University of Phoenix. She received much of her ministerial foundation through servitude in her father's ministry (His Abiding Presence Ministries, Waterford, MI). In August 2009, Evangelist Jones received her ministerial license from Pastor, Dr. Marie E. Brice (Pentecostal Church of Deliverance, Baltimore, MD). On July 1, 2012, Renatta Jones was ordained as evangelist by Apostle Trena D. Stephenson of Woman of God Ministries, Inc.

In 2007, Evangelist Jones began her evangelistic work preaching and assisting ministries and non-profit organizations in the Detroit, MI area. Her desire is to aid individuals and families, especially women and children who are in crisis and to act in capacity as a Christian counselor, advocate, and mentor resulting in the development of Just-Blessed Enterprises [an affiliate of WofGod, Inc. a (501c3) organization under the direction of Overseer Trena D Stephenson]. Services offered through Just-Blessed Enterprises include:

- Counseling (marital, family-related, life-coaching, parental encouragement, & youth mentorship)

- Evangelistic Services: i.e. workshops, seminars, revivals and church related engagements.

- Organizational Leadership services.

- Outreach & Community Service

- Mentorship Training

In addition to Evangelist Jones' educational accomplishments and ministerial endeavors, she is a self-help columnist for SOAR Magazine and is writer and poet for JO Magazine. She is also a contributing author for "And He Still Sees" and "He Still Waits" compiled by Apostle Trena D. Stephenson (Daughters of Distinction, LLC & Women of God Ministries). Evangelist Renatta Jones is also a co-host on "The Fullness of God" radio broadcast which currently airs online and in six states. In retrospect, Evangelist Jones remains humbled by her accomplishments, yet maintains her first and more important work is to her family.

To contact Evangelist Renatta Jones direct all correspondence to: nattajblessed@gmail.com. Further information about Just-Blessed Enterprises is available at www.facebook.com/justblessed1 or by visiting wofgod.org.

CHAPTER 2

God Honors Honesty

As I begin to ponder on my spiritual journey, I see the intricate handiwork of God Almighty. God has a delicate way of turning everything around for our good. The Word of God reads *"And we know that in all things God works for the good of those who love him, who have been called according to his purpose."* (**Romans 8:28 NIV**). These past few years have been pinnacle in my spiritual growth. Now, through Christ I understand the process of becoming a warrior. My life is purpose driven to walk in the image and likeness of Christ offering what I call CPR (Christ Purposed Resurrection) to the multitudes. I humbly recognized that I was once irretrievably broken, or so I thought. *"The LORD is close to the brokenhearted and saves those who are crushed in spirit."* (**Psalm 34:18 NIV**).

One must be aware that you must be whole; before you can heal brokenness in your brother or sister in Christ. I suffered many losses; however, they have molded my character and elevated my perseverance. Many people desire the blessings of God, failing to understand that suffering is significant to increasing your anointing. As a child, growing up, I always felt that there was something different about me. I enjoyed vacation bible school and to this day, I am grateful that my mother sent us. My mother did the best she could with what she had available to her. I was raised in a small town residing in close proximity with my half brothers and sisters. You see I was the bastard child of a married man. For a long time, I walked around feeling like I didn't know who I really was.

This attitude was reinforced by the oppressive words my mother spoke frequently over my life. No matter what, I always had a deep love and concern for my mother. A love that exists today despite the many obstacles we have endured in our tumultuous relationship. I felt a constant void often wondering what my father's favorite color was or whether or not he loved me and my brother. I will never know the answers to those questions because he died when I was a toddler. It was hard riding the school bus with my half siblings teasing, taunting and pulling my hair. Everyday seemed to be an uphill battle.

Sometimes, I think that is why my oldest brother became so angry. He was my protector, courageously saving me from almost being raped by my half-brother. I was oblivious to why he had unzipped my shorts and forcefully held me down. It was overwhelming to hear that he had raped another family member just weeks later. I remember sobbing for her and thinking, now, I understand what he was trying to do to me. My brother and I never spoke of that day until we became adults and reminisced about childhood events. God used my brother to save me from the wiles of the enemy. I could have easily been like Tamar whose brother Amnon became so vexed that he fell sick for his sister desecrating her body **II Samuel 13:1-21**. Rape is an incomprehensible act inflicting the will of someone on a person without their permission. While I was blessed to be sheltered from being raped as a child, the deception of emotional and spiritual rape took residence. The enemy would always use those closest to me to break my spirit. As a teenager, I contemplated suicide many times after debilitating episodes with my mother citing indignations. By the time, I was 17 years old; my first boyfriend punched my driver side car window out on my face. I sat there screaming with pieces of shattered glass lodged throughout my face. The only experience I knew was that love hurt. It wasn't love unless they treated you okay sometimes and abused you ever so often.

Walking into womanhood, I carried the anger, abandonment, resentment and low self-esteem from childhood thus, entering into relationships that were unhealthy. I was abused physically and emotionally by those who were supposed to love and support me. I had battle scars such as fractured bones in my face, black eyes, a severed pinky finger and other visible markings. I had no concept of my own self-worth back then. It baffled me how everyone I came into close relationship with purposed to break my spirit through the power of words. The tongue is one of the greatest weapons used since the creation of mankind. *"Likewise, the tongue is a small part of the body, but it makes great boasts. Consider what a great forest is set on fire by a small spark. The tongue also is a fire, a world of evil among the parts of the body. It corrupts the whole body, sets the whole course of one's life on fire, and is itself set on fire by hell. All kinds of animals, birds, reptiles and sea creatures are being tamed and have been tamed by mankind, but no human being can tame the* tongue. It is a restless evil, full of deadly poison. With the tongue we praise our Lord and Father, and with it we curse human beings, who have been made in God's likeness. Out of the same mouth come praise and cursing. My brothers and sisters, this should not be."(**James 3:5-10 NIV**).

I think the hardest thing to do after suffering emotional abuse is learning to renew your mind daily. Even today, I have to thwart off negative thoughts by speaking the Word of God over my life. Long after the physical injuries have healed, emotional pain seeps into the depths of one's soul. Incidentally, I married the same familiar oppressive spirit that I grew up with. Many people, who grow up in dysfunctional environments, end up having difficulties in relationships as adults. They tend to create chaos in order to resume some sense of normalcy. Sometimes, it seemed like I was on a never ending roller coaster ride.

Then, as I grew more in the knowledge of Jesus Christ, I sometimes was hurt by the brethren in the church. How could this be in the House of God? I soon learned that going to a different church or staying home wasn't the answer to this problem. After all, there is something going on in all places of worship. This isn't intended to speak against attending church, only to be honest that you run from church to church until you learn how to stand. You must stand even in the midst of adversity. We must mature as a body of believers and intercede in prayer for the body of Christ.

I began to ask myself, how much was I really willing to suffer? Jesus already paid it all on the cross. I weathered many storms and cried many tears. I reminded myself of the suffering servant. However, change didn't come until I was completely ready to allow

God to heal me from the pain from the past. Sometimes, we aren't ready to let go of relationships or things that we know aren't edifying who we are to ourselves or God. I found the power of prayer in some of my darkest hours. I called upon the Lord in my secret place and He heard my cry. The Word says, that the Lord, *"sent out his word and healed them; he rescued them from the grave."* (**Psalm 107:20 NIV**).

God's infallible written word leaped off the pages to the preacher's mouth to restore my soul. His love awakened my spirit. Today, I am no longer a bastard seed but a Son of the living God. *"But when the set time had fully come, God sent his Son, born of a woman, born under the law, to redeem those under the law, that we might receive adoption to sonship. Because you are his sons, God sent the Spirit of his Son into our hearts, the Spirit who calls out, "Abba,] Father." So you are no longer a slave, but God's child; and since you are his child, God has made you also an heir."* (**Galatians 4:4-7 NIV**).

The bible is full of the patriarchs of old who were all wrestling with some personal issues. God used these noble examples to demonstrate the power of His spirit to transform man. The transformation of man signifies how God can wash away our sins by the Blood of Jesus. I had to learn how to be open and honest with God even about my shortcomings. God honors honesty. "This is what the LORD says:

"Maintain justice and do what is right, for my salvation is close at hand and my righteousness will soon be revealed." (**Isaiah 56:1 NIV**).

Honesty is the only policy that God will accept. Honesty is personal and sometimes painful. We all know that the truth hurts but it shall set you free. He allowed me to see the role that I played in allowing others to abuse me. I also saw their role and trained myself to stop taking on guilt and responsibility for the sins of others.

"Finally, all of you, be like-minded, be sympathetic, love one another, be compassionate and humble. Do not repay evil with evil or insult with insult. On the contrary, repay evil with blessing, because to this you were called so that you may inherit a blessing. For, "Whoever would love life and see good days must keep their tongue from evil and their lips from deceitful speech. They must turn from evil and do good; they must seek peace and pursue it." (**I Peter 3:8-11 NIV**).

It is God's desire that His children live peaceably with all men. I desperately needed to forgive myself and others in order to walk in complete victory. So I began to examine all that I went through going back and making amends with others. I know some of you are wondering why I went back to those who committed terrible offenses against me? Well, through humility, God has taught me how to love my enemies. I learned how to *"put to death, therefore, whatever belongs to your earthly nature: sexual immorality, impurity, lust, evil desires and greed, which is idolatry. Because of these, the wrath of God is coming. You used to walk in these ways, in the life you once lived. But now you must also rid yourselves of all such things as these: anger, rage, malice, slander, and filthy language from your lips. Do not lie to each other, since you have taken off your old self with its practices and have put on the new self, which is being renewed in knowledge in the image of its Creator."* (**Colossians 3:5-10 (NIV)**.

It takes humility and the Spirit of Christ to offer forgiveness and love to those who have hurt you. I have found that loving your enemies with a pure heart sabotages the end results of what the enemy was attempting to accomplish. God fully examines the intent of a man's heart, for out of it flows the issues of life. Jesus was aware that He had an enemy called Judas who would betray Him for thirty pieces of silver. Jesus knew that Judas was only part of the plan to fulfilling the promise. You must forgive others, regardless, of the sins they have committed against you. *"But I tell you that anyone who is angry with a brother or sister will be subject to judgment. Again, anyone who says to a brother or sister, 'Raca,' is answerable to the court. And anyone who says, 'You fool!' will be in danger of the fire of hell. "Therefore, if you are offering your gift at the altar and there remember that your brother or sister has something against you, leave your gift there in front of the altar. First go and be reconciled to them; then come and offer your gift."* (**Matthew 5:22-24 NIV**).

Reconciliation doesn't mean you have to enter back into relationship with them. It could be as simple as ending conflict or sins being absolved. Otherwise, as the victim, they continue to maintain power and control over your life. I recognize that the enemy used those who hurt me to thrust me closer to my destiny. In the beginning, I ran from the call, not fully comprehending the levity of it. Today, I answer the call with humility and patience waiting as God completes His infinite work in me. I see that I was chosen before the foundations of the world and I had no choice in the election.

"You are my witnesses," declares the LORD, "and my servant whom I have chosen, so that you may know and believe me and understand that I am he. Before me no god was formed, nor will there be one after me. I, even I, am the LORD, and apart from me there is no Savior. I have revealed and saved and proclaimed—I, and not some

foreign god among you. You are my witnesses," declares the LORD, "that I am God. Yes, and from ancient days I am he. No one can deliver out of my hand. When I act, who can reverse it?" (**Isaiah 43:10-13 NIV**).

Nobody can reverse the plan of God. So, embrace the struggles that have helped you grow into the strong individual you are. Today, I know my self-worth and how to set healthy boundaries. I am healed and finally found my voice. Don't judge others by their past or failures. God specializes in making something out of what seems to be nothing. Pray that God will lead and guide them for He knows the plans He has for us to give us an expected end (**Jeremiah 29:11**). Release all the anger, guilt and pain from your past. Embrace the future God has in store for you.

Father, help me to release all pain that I might be completely free. The hurt, guilt, and loneliness heal it, fix it, and deliver my soul. Calm the wind of anger that rages from within me. Help me identify the root of my anger, bitterness, and unforgiveness. Father, it is not Your will that I be angry or consumed. For Your word states: to be angry and sin not. Precious Father, forgive me and those who hurt me. For what right do I have to contend with your will concerning my life? I declare that You are Lord, in the midst of everything. You, God, are my strength and unspeakable joy. In You, I have hope and peace. Father, I have a righteous anger but I will stand still and let You do the warring on my behalf. In Jesus Name. Amen.

MINISTER LYNNEL COPES-PARKER

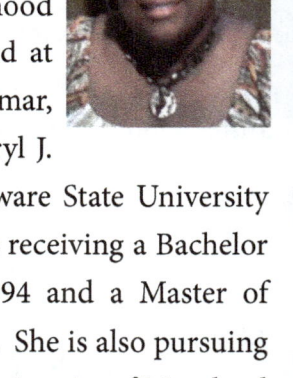

Minister Lynnel Copes-Parker was born and raised on the Lower Eastern Shore of Maryland. She has four daughters Alexus, Kayla, Briana and Leah. Minister Lynnel answered the call to sainthood 18 years ago. She was ordained and licensed at New Beginning Covenant Ministries in Delmar, Delaware under the leadership of Bishop Daryl J. Butts. Minister Lynnel matriculated at Delaware State University and the University of Maryland Eastern Shore receiving a Bachelor of Science degree in Criminal Justice in 1994 and a Master of Education in Guidance in Counseling in 1996. She is also pursuing a doctorate in Educational Leadership at the University of Maryland Eastern Shore. Minister Lynnel has a Bachelor of Biblical Studies, Master of Divinity and Doctorate of Theology from H.E. Wood Bible Institute & Theological Seminary International.

CHAPTER 3

Press Toward Honesty

"There are six things that God hates, seven that are detestable to him. Haughty eyes A lying tongue Hands that shed innocent blood 18A heart that devises wicked schemes Feet that is quick to rush into evil A false witness who pours out lies and A person who stirs up conflict in the community" - (**Proverbs 6:16:19 NIV**)

"For there are six things that God hates—no, seven Haughtiness Lying Murdering Plotting evil Eagerness to do wrong A false witness Sowing discord among brothers" -- (**Proverbs 6:16:19 The Living Bible TLB**)

What is honesty?

Honesty refers to a facet of moral character and connotes positive and virtuous attributes such as integrity, truthfulness and straightforwardness along with the absence of lying, cheating or theft. Is it important to be honest? In today's society, honesty and integrity can be difficult to find. It is considered as something necessary to get by in this world. The bible teaches that we must be honest in speech and conduct. Our honesty has a tremendous impact on people. We honor God and build trust with people when we tell the truth. There are many verses in the Bible that are designed to give us a better understanding of the concept of integrity and honesty. Thomas Jefferson once said, "Honesty is the first chapter in the book of wisdom." *"Living a life that is long and good, watch your tongue, keep your lips from telling lies. Turn away from evil and do good. Work hard at living in peace with one another. The eyes of the Lord watch over those who do right."* (**Psalm 34:13-15 TLB**). Lying destroys integrity. In the case of King Saul and the prophet Samuel (**I Samuel 15:1-35**), Saul thought that he had won a great victory over the Amalekites, but God saw it as a great failure because Saul had disobeyed Him and then lied to Samuel about the results of the battle. Saul defeats the Amalekites, but spares their King. King Saul may have thought his lie would not be detected, or that what he did was not wrong. He lost the ability to tell the difference between truth and lies. By believing your own lies you are deceiving yourself. When individuals tell a lie, usually they find they have to tell further lies to cover the first one. King Saul said that the soldiers were the ones who took the sheep and cattle. They saved the best for the Lord; so they would have something to sacrifice.

God deserves and expect honesty. He delights in our honesty. *"The Lord hates cheating and delights in honesty."* (**Proverbs 11:1 TLB**). *"To do what is right and just is more acceptable to the Lord than sacrifice."* (**Proverbs 21:3 NIV**). God wants us to have a character, which upholds the highest standards of honesty. According to Scripture, virtually everything that truly qualifies a person for leadership is directly related to character. It's not about style, status, personal charisma, clout, or worldly measurements of success.

Integrity is the main issue that makes the difference between a good leader and a bad one." "Integrity is built by defeating the temptation to be dishonest; humility grows when we refuse to be prideful; and endurance develops every time you reject the temptation to give up." There is an inspiring story, titled *"The Seed of Honesty."*

"A successful business man was growing old and knew it was time to choose a successor to take over the business. Instead of choosing one of his Directors or his children, he decided to do something different. He called all the young executives in his company together. He said, "It is time for me to step down and choose the next CEO. I have decided to choose one of you. "The young executives were shocked, but the boss continued." I am going to give each one of you a SEED today – one very special SEED. I want you to plant the seed, water it and come back here one year from today with what you have grown from the seed I have given you. I will judge the plants that you bring, and the one I choose will be the next CEO." One man, named Jim, was there that day and he, like the others, received a seed. He went home and excitedly, told his wife the story. She helped him get a pot, soil and compost and he planted the seed. Every day, he would water it and watch to see if it had grown. After about three weeks, some of the other executives began to talk about their seeds and the plants that were beginning to grow. Jim kept checking his seed, but nothing ever grew. Three weeks, four weeks, five weeks went by, still nothing.

By now, others were talking about their plants, but Jim didn't have a plant and he felt like a failure. Six months went by—still nothing in Jim's pot. He just knew he had killed his seed. Everyone else had tall plants, but he had nothing. Jim didn't say anything to his colleagues, however. He just kept watering and fertilizing the soil—He so wanted the seed to grow. A year finally went by and all the young executives of the company brought their plants to the CEO for inspection. Jim told his wife that he wasn't going to take an empty pot. But she asked him to be honest about what happened. Jim felt sick to his stomach, it was going to be the most embarrassing moment of his life, but he knew his wife was right. He took his empty pot to the board room. When Jim arrived, he was amazed at the variety of plants grown by the other executives. They were beautiful – in all shapes and sizes. Jim put his empty pot on the floor and many of his colleagues laughed, a few felt sorry for him!

When the CEO arrived, he surveyed the room and greeted his young executives. Jim just tried to hide in the back. "My, what great plants, trees, and flowers you have grown," said the CEO. Today one of you will be appointed the next CEO!" All of a sudden, the CEO spotted Jim at the back of the room with his empty pot. He ordered the Financial Director to bring him to the front. Jim was terrified. He thought, "The CEO knows I'm a failure! Maybe he will have me fired. When Jim got to the front, the CEO asked him what had happened to his seed – Jim told him the story. The CEO asked everyone to sit down except Jim. He looked at Jim, and then announced to the young executives, "Behold, your next Chief Executive Officer!

His name is Jim!" Jim couldn't even grow his seed. "How could he be the new CEO?" the others said. Then the CEO said, "One year ago today, I gave everyone in this room a seed. I told you to take the seed, plant it, and water it, and bring it back to me today. But I gave you all boiled seeds; they were dead – it was not possible for them to grow. All of you, except Jim, have brought me trees and plants and flowers. When you found that the seed would not grow, you substituted another seed for the one I gave you. Jim was the only one with the courage and honest to bring me a pot with my seed in it. Therefore, he is the one who will be the new Chief Executive Officer!"

- If you plant honesty, you will reap trust

- If you plant goodness, you will reap friends

- If you plant humility, you will reap greatness

- If you plant perseverance, you reap contentment

- If you plant consideration, you will reap perspective

- If you plant forgiveness, you will reap reconciliation

- If you plant faith in God, you will reap a harvest

So, be careful what you plant now; it will determine what you will reap later."

God delights in men that deal truthfully. *"The Lord detests lying lips but He delights in men who are trustworthy."* (**Proverbs 12:22 NIV**). Let us learn to be truthful, respectful and reverence the Lord, so that, *"The Lord prolongs one's days."* (**Proverbs 10:27 AMP**). It is imperative for Christians to never pay back evil for evil. Do things in such a way that everyone can see you are honest clear through (**Romans 12:17**). Never pay back evil for evil to any man. Remember, that being cruel to others, hurts yourself, but being kind to others, helps you. A kindhearted man will reap blessings from

God, but a cruel man reaps nothing but trouble. *"Your own soul is nourished when you are kind; it is destroyed when you are cruel. The evil man gets rich for the moment, but the good man's reward last forever. The good man finds life; the evil man, death."* (**Proverbs 11:17-19 TLB**).

Considering the times we're living, it's high time to wake up, because our lives might end sooner than we think. If it was important for us to have a relationship with God through Jesus Christ when we first became believers, it's much more important now. The night of sin is coming to an end and the dawn of God's eternal morning will follow. So, throw away everything belonging to the darkness of this world and take up the armor of light. Conduct yourselves honestly, as people do in the daytime. Don't get involved in those things that people like to do in the dark, such as carousing, drunkenness, sensuality of all kinds, sexual orgies, fighting and jealousies.

"Put on the robe of Christ's righteousness and don't do as others whose constant effort in life is to satisfy the cravings of their sinful human nature." (**Romans 13: 14 Clear Word Bible CWB**). God commands us to take off the works of darkness and put on the armor of light. We need to walk decently and well behaved. Stop reveling and drinking. Quit all immoral living. Refrain from quarrelling, contention, and jealousies. Clothe yourself with the character of Jesus Christ (To clothe yourself with Christ interest; to enter into His views and imitating Him in all things). Make no provision for lust

Let's do as Paul says, *"Because of the privilege and authority God has given me, I give each of you this warning: Don't think you are better than you really are. Be honest in your evaluation of yourselves, measuring yourselves by the faith God has given us."*

(**Romans 12:3 New Living Translation NLT**). *"Finally, brethren, whatever things are true, whatever things are honest, whatever things are just, whatever things are pure, whatever things are lovely, whatever things are of good report, if there be any virtue, and if there be any praise, think on these things."* (**Philippians 4:8 TLB**).

Watch your thoughts, for they become words

Watch your words for, they become actions

Watch your actions, for they becomes habits

Watch your habits, for they becomes character

Watch your character, for it becomes your destiny.

(Author – Unknown)

Summarizing it all up friends, I would say you'll do best by filling your minds and meditating on things true, noble, reputable, authentic, compelling, gracious—the best not the worse; to praise not things to curse. Do that, and God who makes everything work together, will work you into His most excellent harmonies. So fix your thoughts on what is true, good and right. Think on things that are pure and lovely. Dwell on the fine, good things in others. Think about all you can praise God for and be glad about. Keep putting into practice all you learn about being honest by following in Christ's footsteps. Knowing that Christ is the Way, the Truth and the Life. Continue to press toward honesty.

PRAYER

Father, I thank you for sending your only Son, Jesus Christ, our Savior, who is the Way, the Truth and the Life. May Your peace, Lord, always be with us, as we press and continue to press toward honesty. Keep our eyes, our mind and our hearts focused and fixed on Christ Jesus. Let not our heart's become deceitful. Holy Spirit help us to walk in truth and always ready to receive from the Lord, His principles, His ways, His understanding and His wisdom. Lord Jesus, as Your mandate was to please the Father, help us to follow in the same mandate for our lives, which belong to You. Help us to live a life that is pleasing with honesty, truth, holiness and righteousness. Always, doing the will of our Father. In Jesus Mighty Precious Name. Amen.

MINISTER NANCY J. DUCKETT

Minister Nancy J. Duckett serves as an associate minister, under the leadership of Bishop Dwayne C. Debnam, at Morning Star Baptist Church, in Catonsville, MD. She is currently attending Washington Bible College in pursue of her theology degree. She is also a 2010 graduate of the International Liturgical Dance Fellowship and Academy. She serves as a facilitator at Adult Church School, Discipleship, New Members Classes and ministers in the prisons and nursing homes. In 1996, God called her to form a Discipleship Class at her workplace the Social Security Administration, which is still active today after her retirement in 2010.

Minister Duckett values family very highly. She is the mother of four blessed, gifted and anointed sons, two wonderful, blessed and gifted anointed daughter-in-laws, grandmother of six beautiful blessed grandchildren, and a great-grandmother of two beautiful blessed great-grandchildren.

CHAPTER 4

Alone in a Room

"Because of the privilege and authority God has given me, I give each of you this warning: Don't think you are better than you really are. Be honest in your evaluation of yourselves, measuring yourselves by the faith God has given us." (**Romans 12:3 NLT**)

We are about to embark on a journey to the discovery of the true meaning of honesty. I want you to take a few moments to imagine a few things. You arrive home from work after an exhausting day in the office. There is no television on, no cellphones ringing, and no emails to read. The truth is you don't have the strength to do anything, even if your life depended on it. You begin to disrobe as you prepare for a bath. You catch a glimpse of a person in the mirror that you don't quit seem to recognize. You think to yourself; "Do I know her from somewhere?" Then a weird feeling comes over you. I don't know this person at all. Without the make-up and clothes, the person in the mirror is a stranger.

Many of us have hidden behind fancy clothes, make-up and

successful careers for years. You have no idea who you are without these things. It is difficulty to be alone with this person. We have lived a life full of so many lies that we have gotten caught up in our own hype. The stories about our lives are so grand that we are now superstars in our own sitcom; "The Real Life of the Perfect Person." We are in character on the stage of life, arrayed with all the designer clothes, stage make-up and perfectly edited script of righteous conversation. But then the lights go down, and wardrobe packs up, you have to go home. It is just you, alone in a room. What is a Christian to do? God desires to spend time with you. You scramble to find your script but there is none to be found. You begin to try to pray, but the words escape you. You try to recall the dynamic words uttered in prayer by Pastor on last Sunday. You were hoping to use those words to get it right. But you just begin to mumble through, speaking words that make no sense at all. Something in that quiet room, brushes pass your face and sits down on the bed beside you. He whispers in your ear, "take off the mask, lay down your role and come to me with a pure heart." *"Who shall ascend into the hill of the Lord? Or who shall stand in his holy place? We that hath clean hands and a pure heart, who hath not lifted up his soul unto vanity nor sworn deceitfully. He shall receive the blessing from the Lord and righteousness from the God of his salvation."* (**Psalms 24 3-5 KJV**). It is time to be honest with God, and yourself.

I have spent many years being dishonest with myself. I was too afraid to live the life God called me to; but terrified to die without having God's purpose fulfilled. I got dressed each day with my outer garments pressed and neatly arranged to depict the character of Christ, but my spirit man was filthy dirty. I thought I could "fake it, until I made it" but boy was I wrong. I found myself having to provide explanations for my action, decisions or lack thereof. My responses were often harsh, blunt and hurtful to the receiver. I was just being "honest." By standing on a portion of the definition of honesty, I delivered blow after blow to family, friends or anyone that got in my way. I left a path of destruction everywhere I went. This was a defense mechanism used to protect my story. What if my secrets were to get out? How would I explain it? It would hurt too bad to honestly tell the story.

This dishonesty led me farther and farther from God. God became a vague distant memory. I could remember personal contact with Him as a child. However, I stopped spending time with Him years ago. I didn't trust myself, and surely not some distant God; the one I held responsible for all the pain and disappointments that I endured. Praying became some religious act that I did just to impress others when called upon, or when I was facing an unbearable trouble. I had the mindset, "God knows what is going on; so, if He wants to fix it then He will." The truth of the matter was I have been so dishonest with myself that I did not know what the truth was anymore.

I told and demonstrated lie after lie in the story of my life, until one day the heavenly father began to deal mightily with me. He began to allow circumstances and situations to arise that left me with no other option but to turn to Him. Of course, many of those initial prayers were just religious exercise with little to no spiritual sincerity. I needed help and I knew from a past relationship with God that He was the only one who could help. Each encounter with God stripped off a layer of dishonesty. The stripping would leave some raw exposed areas on my heart. I attempted to cover them with make-up and clothes, but the blood and pain leaked out. As a nurse for many years, I am familiar with a procedure called debridement. This procedure is necessary to assist with wound healing. During the procedure, the doctor cuts away the dead tissue that is preventing a wound from healing properly. This procedure, in turn, makes the wound deeper, and the wound usually bleeds more. This is when the healing process can begin. God uses a similar process with us to begin healing our hearts.

"A new heart also will I give you, and a new spirit will I put within you: and I will take away the stony heart out of your flesh, and I will give you a heart of flesh." (**Ezekiel 36:26 KJV**).

This is actually, what God began to do in my life. He began cutting away at the scabs that grew because of obesity, low self-esteem, fornication, adultery, divorce, bitterness, and hatred. All of these things were attached to my heart. I tried to cover them with fine clothes, jewelry, make-up and a successful career. But the stench from my dying spirit would seep out when I thought I was being honest with others. My words would cut them to their core.

"Let us walk honestly, as in the day, not in rioting, and drunkenness: not in chambering and wantonness, not in strife and envying." (**Romans 13:13 KJV**)

The Greek word for honestly is euschemonos, which means becomingly or decently. God is instructing the church to uncover all the dark deeds of your past, and present. In Psalms 24: 3-4, David speaks of having "clean hands, and a pure heart" as the key to being able to dwell and have relationship with God. Honesty is valued by God. He is looking for someone that does not tell or live lies. This includes telling a half-truth that omits part of the details, which

Daughters of Distinction

leads to deception. It is impossible to have a relationship with God when you are dishonest. Honesty is a direct reflection of your inner character.

According to Merriam-Webster, honesty means fairness and straightforwardness of conduct. With closer examination, it also refers to a moral character and is associated with positive, virtuous attributes such as integrity, truthfulness, trustworthy, loyal, veracity, fair and sincere. When you begin to allow God to cleanse your hands and purify your heart, you will begin to be able to have open communication with Him.

The fear of loss and rejection is typically the root cause of dishonesty. This fear causes you to re-write the story of your life. You take the roles of writer, producer, and actor. You begin to serve yourself, making all the props needed for your story idols. These props include your career, mate, money, and worldly processions. The props become little "gods" in your life. God has given us the commandment that *"thou shall not have any other gods before me."* **(Exodus 20:3 KJV)**

Be grateful that God is a forgiving God. He has given us the opportunity to repent. Take off the mask (be honest), wash your clothes (repent), and put on the full armor of God (be restored). The time of Christ's return is fast approaching. We must not waste any more time trying to obtain things and impress people. We must get up and develop a mindset to be about God's business. It is our responsibility to share the gospel of Jesus Christ with the world. But in order to do it, you must be honest with yourself, and God. Refuse to allow fear to get the victory. As you begin to clothe yourself in honesty, you will begin to take on the character of Christ. The nature of your thought life will change. God is able to work through you to save others. You are able to go to the Father without shame. Many people use the cliché, "so as a man thinketh, so is he." This is the truth, based on the scripture in **Proverbs 23:7**. You must renew your mind on a daily basis. Honest thoughts will open the door to a pure relationship with God. He will begin to deal with each area, one at a time.

You can lay down your role and allow God to direct your life. Begin the journey to an effective prayer life, by being honest with God about how you feel, and where you are with regards to your relationship with Him. As you yield to the process, God will be able to deliver you into your divine purpose and destiny in Christ. Now, is the time to be honest.

Father, I pray that every person that would pick up this book will allow You to cleanse all the wounds in their hearts. Heal all their pain, deliver them from their past. Father, cause them to take an honest look at themselves. In this examination, show them all the areas that have hindered their relationship with You. Once you have dug out all the dead tissue, apply your healing balm. In the places of past hurts, pack it with Your love. Father, I declare deliverance from fraud, deception, dishonesty, fear, and reject over the lives of the reader. I decree that they shall have a renewed mind, joy unspeakable, a peace that surpasses their understanding. I am thankful that you are able to do exceedingly, abundantly above all I can ever ask. I stand believing that you will do a mighty work in the life of the reader, in the name of Jesus, Amen.

TONOAH P. HAMPTON

Tonoah P. Hampton is the CEO and founder of Pursuing Destiny LLC. The vision of Pursuing Destiny LLC was placed in her heart in 2005. Its commitment is to helping hurting and disadvantaged people achieve optimal health and wellness.

She is a registered nurse and a health and wellness coach. She spends her time educating and coaching people about holistic health and wellness. She is able to provide sound life changing information that helps facilitate the realization of God's original plan and purpose for their life.

Tonoah has faced many challenges, such as sexual assault, divorce, low self- esteem and obesity. With the grace of God, she has been able to overcome them all. She has realized that each challenge was an opportunity for God to get His glory from life. The challenges weren't just for her benefit but for all those that God would send her way. She is passionate about helping others achieve optimal health and wellness: mind, body and spirit.

She had been searching for a spiritual covering for several years since moving to Baltimore, MD. The Lord was faithful and led her to Kingdom Life Church, where Michael Phillips is the pastor. It is the mission of Kingdom Life Church to help people live a better life.

Her most prized job is that of being the wife of H. Lamonte Hampton and mother of their six children. One of her greatest accomplishments though personal, is her 150-pound weight loss. "Be strong and of a good courage..." Joshua 1:6 has guided her to achieving and maintaining this success.

She has accomplished so much over the years. She continues to inspire others in her quest to promote change in their minds, bodies, and spirits. She has held such titles as Mrs. Christian International, Mrs. Christian United States, and Mrs. North American Essence. She attributes all of her success to God. Without God none of these things would have been possible.

Tonoah has recently accepted her God-given destiny and launched a health and wellness coaching company. Pursuing Destiny LLC is the fulfillment of a lifelong dream of helping propel people into their destiny. Pursuing Destiny LLC is where inner healing leads to the manifestation of optimal health and wellness.
In Pursuit of destiny, one purposeful step at a time.

CHAPTER 5

Honesty

"Let us go boldly unto the throne of grace that we may obtain mercy and find grace to help in the time of need" (**Hebrews 4:16 KJV**).

To be effective in prayer, we must realize to whom we are praying and we must realize that prayer is a two-way street. We should not be doing all of the talking, but we should also listen for what God is saying to us; through our spirit, the Word, or godly people. We are praying to the great I Am; the One and only true God; creator of heaven and earth; merciful, kind, and gracious Father who is forgiving and who loves us enough to dwell (live) within and among us. God is patient with us, for truly we are not always an obedient people. Yet, it is His patience and mercy that helps to mold us into the image of His Son, Jesus Christ. God's gentleness makes us great and helps in the molding department. His gentleness allows us to grow and to receive correction; it allows us to fall and get up so we can learn from our mistakes.

So, now that we realize to whom we are speaking, we need to focus on how we are to approach God—in Honesty. The Encarta Dictionary defines honesty as moral uprightness—the quality, condition, or characteristic of being fair, truthful, and morally upright; and truthfulness (candor or sincerity). There can be no honesty apart from God. The world looks at morality as a relative thing. Morals depend on what is acceptable to society at the time. For example, pregnancy out of wedlock was immoral at one time, now it is accepted as the norm. True morality (the righteousness that comes from God) has been substituted for what "is politically correct." I think we confuse God's forgiveness, for acceptability. God may forgive us of sin, but that doesn't mean the sin is acceptable.

Honesty is a matter of the heart. We can speak the truth but if our heart/our motives are not truthful, then we have corrupted the truth—we are not operating or praying in honesty. Scripture says *"we have not because we ask not, and when we ask, we ask amiss that we may consume it upon our own lusts."* (**James 4:2b-3 KJV**). In other words, our motives are wrong. For example: for years I prayed for the salvation of my husband, but I desired it for my convenience (so, I would not continue to go through heartache) and as my "trophy" (proof that I was a good Christian wife)—not because I really saw the need of his soul. I walked this ways for years, until God revealed to me that my motives were wrong. I repented and I released him to God. I realized that my trust had to be in God and not in the visible manifestation of his salvation. In God's time, he received Christ. And as I continue to pray for his growth, I am reminded to check my motives in prayer and let God, not me, have His way in him.

We must recognize that God knows all things. He knows our thoughts, our heart, and our motives. We must come before Him bare, with our layers removed—no hiding from the truth—and we confess to Him. God desires truth in our inward parts (**Psalm 51:6a**). He already knows where we are, but when we come to Him in truth, He accepts our prayers.

In order, to walk or come to God in truth, we must come with no hidden agendas. One of my life desires is the desire for purity. I have adopted a definition of purity, which says "I will not manipulate, pre-program, or project any hidden agendas onto anyone or anything." I used to think that meant I should not have an agenda, but I've come to realize that my agenda should be the same as God's agenda—to save souls. We must be transparent, not only with God but with each other. We must examine the motives behind our prayers and our actions.

"Keep thy heart with all diligence, for out of it are the issues of life." (**Proverbs 4:23 KJV**). We are compelled to examine ourselves to see if we are in the faith. I don't just mean in the "Christian faith," but are we operating in faith? *Whatever is not of faith is sin* (**Romans 14:23b KJV**). We received our salvation, our ticket into the abundant life, through grace by faith in God's Word. Therefore everything we are seeking (every God-given promise) should be obtained the same way-- through grace by faith in God's Word. Our prayers should not be ritualistic, but we should approach the throne in honesty. Look, God already knows what is going on in our hearts, He knows where we stand, our agenda. The best thing we can do is come before Him honestly with a broken and contrite (repentant) spirit. *"The sacrifices of God are a broken spirit: a broken and a contrite heart, O God, thou wilt not despise."* (**Psalm 51:17 KJV**). *"The Lord is nigh unto them that are of a broken heart; and saves such as be of a contrite spirit."* (**Psalm 34:18 KJV**). Try as we might, we can't hide

the truth from God.

I believe honesty is a by-product of the fruit of the Spirit. For when you operate in love, joy, peace, longsuffering, gentleness, goodness, faith, meekness (you are teachable), and temperance (self-control), it causes you to walk in honesty. It is the fruit of the Spirit that shows if you are developing godly character. You cannot operate in the fruit half-heartedly or with ulterior motives; it will be evident to most that your character is not godly—you are not really loving, joyous, etc. **Romans 12:9a (KJV)** says, we are to "let love be without dissimulation." When we operate in dissimulation we disguise or hide true feelings, thoughts, or intentions—we operate in falsehood.

I've found that God will allow things to take place in our lives, so that we will know where we stand. These "things" may be trials, difficulties, heartaches, or even success. When the children of Israel were coming out of the wilderness, God said they were to *"remember all the way which the Lord led them...to humble thee, and to prove thee, to know what was in thine heart, whether thou wouldest keep his commandments or no.."* (**Deuteronomy 8:2 KJV**). There may be areas in our lives that we thought we have dealt with, but when faced with those situations, we find we are still harboring or holding on to some untruths. These "things" (trials, difficulties, heartaches, or successes) help to break up the fallow ground in us (ground that has been plowed but unseeded). Like a farmer breaks up the soil for planting, turning it over and over, and uprooting weeds; so, God uses these difficulties to turn over and uproot the soil of our hearts; so, that every untrue thing in us can be brought to the light of the Gospel. It is only when we bring every hidden and ugly thing to the Light that it is exposed for what it is. God's Word is that light,

Daughters of Distinction

and through the Word we are washed and cleansed (**Ephesians 5:26 KJV**).

The Word of God is the only thing that can change us. When we look into the mirror of the Word, we see ourselves as we are and we see ourselves as God sees us. As we are, we see that we are sinful and are in need of a Savior; we see that our hearts are deceitful and full of wickedness (**Jeremiah 17:9 KJV**). However, once we accept Christ as our Savior and Lord, we are cleansed of our sin and we can see as God sees us by the blood of Jesus—pure, holy, and acceptable.

When Jesus was selecting/calling the disciples, he found Phillip and said "Follow me." Phillip in turn went to Nathanael and said *"We have found him of whom Moses in the law and the prophets wrote, Jesus of Nazareth, the son of Joseph."* Nathanael responded *"Can there any good thing come out of Nazareth?"* Phillip said *"Come and see."* (**John 1:43-46 KJV**). Jesus saw Nathanael coming, and said "Behold an Israelite indeed in whom is no guile" (cunning, deceitful or treacherous quality). (**John 1:47 KJV**). In other words, he was saying here is an honest man. What made Nathanael a man without guile? He spoke what he honestly thought: "Can any good thing come out of Nazareth?"

Now, to be honest, we cannot do this (be honest) in our own strength. There are many times we are tempted to lie, to think of ourselves before others, to cheat in order to get ahead, or to harm someone (in words or deed). However, it is the Holy Spirit (working in us) who restrains us and who causes us to rely on Him for help. When we are tempted to operate in our flesh, it is then that we go before God in all honesty. We confess our limitations and our fleshly desires and ask for His help. *"If we confess our sins, God is faithful and just to forgive us of our sins and cleanse us of all unrighteousness."* (**I John 1:9 KJV**)—but only when we are honest before Him.

Many of the righteous kings and prophets of Israel cried out to God in truth and interceded for the people by confessing the sins of the nation and admitting to their rebelliousness. They asked for God's mercy, and received it (mercy) because of the honest acknowledgement and repentance of their sin. Let us also reverence God as we go before His holy throne in honesty and truth. Sometimes, we think we can't say certain things to God, but remember God already knows what we are thinking. Besides, He is big enough to handle anything we bring before him—He won't be offended with our statements. Let's honor Him by being honest with Him.

Some years ago, I went through a devastating period in ministry of betrayal, hurt, and confusion. The leadership walked away from the Word of God and in turn corrupted the thinking of some of the membership. This resulted in me walking away from organized religion, and mistrusting preachers. As I prayed to God in my hurt, I said God you already knew this was going to happen; why did you let us go through this, why didn't you warn us? In my anguish, I learned an important truth: "Keep your eyes on God and don't put your trust in the arm of flesh." We are all subject to fall, because we are in flesh. But God never fails. After a thorough examination, I realized He had warned me but I trusted man. The Word my former pastor preached was truth, but her lifestyle didn't match the Word. <u>Honesty is integrity in our actions, not just in our words</u>.

As I was raising my three daughters, there is one thing I always reiterated to them: "If you lie, you will get a far worse punishment than if you simply tell the truth." I believe God feels the same way. Remember, *"He desires truth in the inward parts and in the hidden parts he shall make us to know wisdom."* (**Psalm 51:6 KJV**).

"So let us go boldly (honestly) unto the throne of grace that we may obtain mercy and find grace to help (us) in the time of need." (**Hebrews 4:16 KJV**).

Father God, You alone have created us and you know every intimate detail of our lives. You see beyond our outward appearances—Lord, You know us inside and out. You know our thoughts, our motives, our desires, and even the intents of our heart—Your Word examines and divides these things. Forgive us for seeking man's approval over Your approval; forgive us for fearing man (which is a snare) but not fearing You; forgive us for our rebelliousness, and our stubbornness; forgive us for not walking in faith. Lord, we are a sinful people, who are selfish, and who think more of ourselves than of others. Lord, we confess that we don't seek after You with our whole heart, we do that which is convenient for us and at times we seek to be politically correct. We ask for Your mercy, Lord.

Our country, which was established with Christian principles, has gone so far from your way. We see the evidence of this in the crime, homosexuality, fornication, covetousness, envy, murder, deceit, and disrespect for parents and authority figures (**Romans 1:18-32**). Lord, you said in II Chronicles 7:14, *"IF my people, which are called by my name, shall humble themselves, and pray, and seek my face, and turn from their wicked ways: THEN will You hear from heaven and will forgive our sins and will heal our land."* (KJV). This prayer is conditional. We must do our part as Christians to allow Your Word

to plow the fallow ground of our hearts that we might bring all things to Your light. Lord, we, who are called by Your name, are crying out to You. Forgive our sins, for they are numerous; and heal our land. Give us repentant hearts that we may come before Your throne in honesty, and once again return to You—our First Love.
In Jesus' Name, Amen.

JACQUELINE CHASE

Jacqueline Chase has been married to Bruce Chase for 39 years. She is the mother of three daughters: Nija, Sheena, and Tiana, and has three grandsons. She was licensed in ministry in 1984 at the Dalton Baptist Church and was a founding member of the now defunct Spirit of Liberty Church in Baltimore, MD.

She has been a member of Mount Pleasant Ministries in Baltimore, MD for over 17 years. When she first came to the Mount, she was spiritually battered and bruised. Under the nurture of the Word and the tender care of Bishop Johnson, she has been healed, spiritually and emotionally and continues to grow in her faith in God.

Jackie served as a co-laborer in the Discipleship ministry for over 10 years in the MasterLife and Survival Kit discipleship programs, and she currently works in the Evangelism ministry. She is a contributing writer for the Mount Pleasant Ministry Update "For Her Eyes Only," a gifted teacher, and is a member of the Women of Worship (W.O.W.) dancers. After working for 40 years, she recently retired from the Social Security Administration where she co-facilitated the Wednesday Bible Study at the National Computer Center.

Most importantly, Jackie is a born again worshiper who loves the Lord Jesus and serves him unashamedly wherever the Lord plants her (on the job, in the home, in her community, and in her church).

CHAPTER 6

The Spirit of Truth

"*Even the Spirit of Truth; whom the world cannot receive, because it seeth him not, neither knoweth him: but ye know him; for he dwelleth with you, and shall be in you.*" (**John 14:17 KJV**). In the preceding scripture, Jesus makes mention of the "The Spirit of Truth" who is the Holy Spirit. The scripture makes clear that it is impossible to know God without knowing the Holy Spirit. Those who truly know God will obey Him and follow His ways by the leading of The Spirit of Truth, but those who do not obey Him, do not know Him are unknowingly led by a demon called "the spirit of error" (**I John 4:6**). With this in mind, I wish to explain the significance of the Spirit of Truth also known as the Holy Spirit and His work. Thus this chapter includes the following subtopics: *Understanding Honesty; Christ's Example of a Life of Honesty; The Secret to living the life of Honesty, and the Purpose of The Spirit of Truth.*

Understanding Honesty

Giving the specific meaning of the word "honesty" is vitally important to ensure there is no misunderstanding in the further discussions of this topic. It is also important that the foundation of this word be clarified because of the belief that honesty only applies to someone demonstrating openness in character by telling his or her personal business. The root word for honesty, honest as defined by Merriam-Webster, means *legitimate, truthful, genuine, real, reputable, respectful, humble, plain, good, worthy, praiseworthy, innocent, and simple.* The definition of "honesty " means *"fairness and straightforwardness of conduct, adherence to the facts: sincerity.* The antonyms for honesty are *deceit, deceitfulness, dishonesty, lying, and untruthfulness.* Furthermore, the Greek word for honesty is "Semnotes" meaning *"The characteristic of a person that entitles him to reverence and respect, dignity, majesty, and sanctity. It is a necessary characteristic of the life and conduct of Christians 1 Timothy 2:2,3 honesty which flows from a life of gravity; a qualification of a bishop or overseer in a church, in regard to his children 1 Timothy 3:4, a necessary characteristic of the teaching imparted by a servant of God, Titus 2:7."*

Christ's Example of a Life of Honesty

To further understand the meaning of honesty, it is necessary to look at the life of Jesus Christ. It is important to emphasize that the life of honesty requires demonstration and is the fruit or work of character transformation. Jesus is the only person who came to earth and lived a perfect and holy life in the sight of His father in heaven. According to scripture, God is light and in Him there is no darkness. Additionally, God cannot lie because it is not in His nature (**1 John 1:5 & Numbers 23:19**). In contrast, Satan is known as the father of sin, as well as, deception. Likewise, his goal is to cause mankind to walk in sin using the lust of the flesh, the lust of the eyes, and the pride of life. Jesus spoke of him in the gospel of **John 8:44 (KJV)** saying, *"Ye are of your father the devil, and the lusts of your father ye will do. He was a murderer from the beginning, and abode not in the truth, because there is no truth in him. When he speaketh a lie, he speaketh of his own: for he is a liar, and the father of it."* The devil is a liar and a deceiver who wishes to steal the breath of life, given to us by God. He wishes to kill us, and to devour us, as a roaring lion (**1 Peter 5:8**).

As a result, of the enemy's deception; mankind fell into sin resulting in the loss of a personal relationship with God. Thus, a curse was placed upon the world and mankind for us to be born into sin. What is sin? Sin is iniquity and the total complete opposite of holiness; it is an act of disobedience and rebellion to the ordinances, commandments, and statutes of God. God cannot dwell where sin exists because He is righteous, just, and holy (**Numbers 14:18, Isaiah 59:2 & Habakkuk 1:13**). However, God wants us to have life everlasting as revealed in His Word by Christ. **John 3:16** states: that God loved the world so much that He gave His one and only Son so that anyone who believes in Him will not die but have eternal life. Jesus came to earth to redeem and save the world from sin because of the fall of Adam and Eve and the iniquity that resulted (**Genesis 1:26-27, Genesis 3 & John 1:29**). Jesus chose to take the sins of the world upon Him so that by grace, faith and through His sacrifice we may become the righteousness of God (**Isaiah 53:4-2 & 2 Corinthians 5:21**). God desires us to live a life of godliness, holiness, and honesty according to His Word in **I Timothy 2:1-3**. To obtain salvation and live as God intended we must first believe on the gospel of Jesus Christ, which is the work He did to deliver mankind from the curse of sin and death. His work includes how He died, was buried, and arose three days later (**1 Corinthians 15:3-4**).

The Secret to living the life of Honesty

Christ Jesus came and walked the earth. He was tempted in every way as the Bible teaches, yet, He was without sin because of submitting Himself unto God His father and resisting the works of the devil (**Matthew 4**). The bible tells us that Christ was born and lived a perfect life by the power of the Holy Ghost.

In **Luke 2:34-35**, the power of the Holy Spirit is evident in the birth of Jesus Christ when the angel Gabriel came to Mary and foretold His birth. In **John 1:1-14**, Jesus is called "The Word." Therefore, it was the person of the Holy Spirit who took "The Word" making and forming Him into a man called Emanuel "God with us." Please understand that Christ Jesus was just as much man as though He were not God, because the Holy Spirit by His own power caused Him to become human. It is the Holy Spirit who impregnated Mary, who was a virgin. It is by Him that Christ never fell into sin. It is also by Him (The Holy Spirit) that Christ healed the sick, raised the dead, and cast out demons. It is because of the Holy Spirit that Jesus could suffer and endure the tremendous horrific beating from the Roman soldiers who took Him to the cross to be crucified. The Holy Spirit is also responsible for raising Jesus from the dead to declare and confirm Him as being the Son of God. Christ could not have accomplished this life or fulfilled His ministry without the power of the Holy Spirit (**Acts 10:38**).

Unfortunately, we as humans both in and out of the body of Christ battle through various struggles such as fornication, drugs, alcohol, pornography, etc. The bible tells us that we cannot live this life of honesty that is called "The Christian Life" without the Holy

Spirit. We cannot do this by our human will because we will fail. In **Zechariah 4:6 (KJV)** the scripture confirms "Not by might, nor by power, but by my spirit, saith the Lord of hosts." The secret to living the life of honesty involves: knowing Jesus as Lord and Savior (**John 3:3-15**); developing a personal relationship with Him by the Holy Spirit (**John 14:26**); and having His Word in our lives (**Psalm 17:4-5 and Psalm 119:11**).

The Spirit of Truth

According to **John 16:13-14**, Jesus refers to the Holy Spirit as "The Spirit of Truth" stating the Holy Spirit guides us into all truth. He glorifies the Son of God and testifies of Him. While Christ was on earth, He was faithful to the Father. Likewise, the Holy Spirit is faithful to the Son of God in that He is in the world today to reveal the gospel of Jesus Christ to all who will receive. The Holy Spirit is also the one who reveals the work of the cross to the hearts of men and women, bringing us to conviction. As a result, we can honestly acknowledge the need for Christ's blood to cleanse us from iniquity (**Psalm 51**). It is by Him that people recognize the need for God's forgiveness. However, when the Holy Spirit comes to change a person's life, He will not force Himself on anyone because He is humble, meek, gentle, and patient but yet powerful. According to I John 1:6, if we say we have fellowship with God and walk in sin we lie and do not live a life of honesty and truth. Verse 10 says that if we say that we do not have any sin in our lives we make God a liar and His Word is not present with us. Therefore, "The Spirit of Truth" is the great revealer; the one who uncovers and unveils. He brings to light what is in darkness to bring justice and hope for deliverance as is reflected in the following parable.

"A sower went out to sow his seed: and as he sowed, some fell by the side; and it was trodden down, and the fowls of the air devoured it. And some fell upon a rock; and as soon as it was sprung up, it withered away, because it lacked moisture. And some fell among thorns; and the thorns sprang up with it, and choked it. And other fell on good ground, and sprang up, and bear fruit an hundredfold....Now the parable is this: The seed is the word of God. Those by the wayside are they that hear; then cometh the devil, and taketh away the word out of their hearts, lest they should believe and be saved. They on the rock are they, which, when they hear, receive the word with joy; and these have no root, which for a while believe, and in time of temptation fall way. And that which fell among thorns are they, which when they have heard, go forth, and are chocked with cares and riches and pleasures of this life, and bring no fruit to perfection. But that on the good ground are they, which in an honest and good heart, having heard the word, keep it, and bring forth fruit with patience." (**Luke 8:5-15 KJV**).

Consequently, the reason the last group of people received the word is the conviction of the Spirit of Truth doing a work in their hearts. He brought to light a need for forgiveness and repentance; so, that they can be renewed and changed into the righteousness of God.

The bible also tells us that the Spirit of Truth is the one who reveals to a person that the man Christ Jesus is the Son of God. In **Matthew 16:13-18 (KJV)**, Jesus asked His disciples whom do men say that I am? They said that some call you John the Baptist, some Elias, some Jeremiah, or one of the prophets, but Jesus said what about you? Who do you say I am? Peter looked at Jesus and said

"Thou art the Christ, the Son of the living God." Jesus responded in saying flesh and blood had not revealed this to you Peter but my Father who is in heaven. It was none other but the Spirit of Truth who brought to light and made known the deity of Christ Jesus unto Peter.

Another example occurs in **Matthew 27:54 (KJV)**, the centurion and those with him saw the crucified Christ hanging dead on the cross. The Bible says that they feared greatly after the sudden earthquake that occurred. They looked up at Jesus after having mocked him on the cross but with a change of heart in saying *"Truly this was the Son of God."* This revelation could only occur to someone by the working and manifestation of the Spirit of Truth. Additionally, in **John I:32-34**, John the Baptist testifies of the revelation he received of Jesus at the Jordan River. He knew the Father, but did not know the Son. Upon seeing Jesus come up out of the waters of baptism, John the Baptist saw the Spirit descending upon Christ in the form of a dove. The scripture says in verse 34 that while he saw and witnessed this he bore record, and he knew that this was the Son of God. Undoubtedly, The Spirit of Truth, who is the power of the Godhead in heaven, is the one that proves, brings to life and manifests the work of Calvary. Therefore, any who doubt the gospel will know assuredly as Jesus said…*"I am the way, the truth, and the life: no man cometh unto the Father, but by me."* (**John 14:6 KJV**).

<u>Conclusion</u>

The word "honesty" means the same as truthfulness. To live a life of honesty requires embracing the Holy Spirit also known as the Spirit of Truth. The Spirit of Truth convicts with The Word to bring sinners to the knowledge of the need for repentance. It is the Holy

Spirit who delivers us from the power of sin. In conclusion, we need the person of the Holy Spirit to live out the full meaning of honesty as unto the Lord.

Father, I come to you in the name of your precious Son Jesus Christ. I pray for every person who has read and will read this chapter that by "The Spirit of Truth" they will come to know the work of the cross. I pray that you will bring salvation, healing, and deliverance to every area of their lives. I rebuke the powers of the devil that would try to come against their lives by the authority and power of the shed blood of Jesus, and I release the anointing of the Holy Ghost that breaks the yoke of bondage and brings restoration to all who read these words. The Lord bless thee and keep thee, the Lord make His face to shine upon thee, and to be gracious unto thee, and the Lord lift His countenance upon thee, and give thee peace. In the name of your Son, I pray. Amen.

PASTOR JONATHAN J.R.W PARNELL

Jonathan J.R.W Parnell is the second of two children born on August 25, 1987 to Pastor Rodney and Janet Parnell. Having accepted the Lord, at an early age and baptized, Jonathan has a passion for the things of God, the bible, and the ministry of the gospel of Jesus Christ. Throughout all his life from the age of five, Jonathan has been deeply touched and influenced by the healing and deliverance ministry of Benny Hinn, Oral Roberts, and Kathryn Kuhlman. As a teenager, Jonathan answered the call of God to the Christian Ministry.

In March 2007, he delivered his first message before an appreciable audience at After Christ Christian Center in Detroit, MI. Subsequently, in June 2009, he was officially licensed to preach the Gospel of our Lord and Savior Jesus Christ by his father. In 2008 he participated with his parents in the making and releasing of their CD called "Are You Ready" a poetic prophetic dramatization of end time poems put to music. Additionally, Jonathan was ordained as Pastor on September 23, 2012. As Jonathan continues his walk, he certainly will further his education both naturally and spiritually in "The Word of God," and fulfill the glorious commission of our Lord and Savior Jesus Christ.

CHAPTER 7

Possessing the Integrity of Joseph

In ones' prayer life, honesty must be a part the prayer assignment. Honesty has other partners, integrity being one of them. Integrity is a part of our character development. It is important to our Christian journey, no matter what the assignment or call. As a prayer warrior, intercessor, or pray-er, specific qualifications are necessary for a successful prayer life. Integrity is one of the qualifications. Integrity does not stand alone, but; is closely related and works hand in hand with honesty. Integrity is defined by Webster as "a state of being complete, unbroken wholeness, state of being unimpaired, perfect condition, and soundness, being of sound moral principle, uprightness, honesty, and sincerity.") We know that we accomplish these traits through Jesus Christ our Lord, as He is only perfect.

Compassion is another necessary ingredient for prayer. Although compassion is foundational for prayer warriors, integrity is equally important in the life of the pray-er. Compassion will lead you to integrity. Integrity is a choice and a growth process. The more we chose integrity in our decision making and actions, the stronger

Daughters of Distinction

we become as prayer warriors and intercessors. The Holy Spirit is our guide and teacher. (**John 14:26**). As we yield to the Holy Spirit, integrity increases. He will notify us when we are incorrect in our actions or thinking.

When one possesses integrity as a partner of honesty, the prayer life has an increased success rate. As integrity and honesty is on board; our prayers are clean, confidential, and penetrating through the powers of darkness. We should desire for our prayers to be answered. Early in my prayer life, I asked God to "fix" me so He would answer my prayers. To further examine the application of integrity in our lives and its effect on prayer and outcome, the biblical character of Joseph's trials and situations are reviewed and discussed. Joseph's integrity, loyalty to God, and honesty was tested many times. Along with these trials, his character grew as he aged (**Genesis chapters 37-50**).

Joseph was born to Rachel and Jacob. He was favored by his father, as he was a child born in Jacob's old age (**Genesis 30:22-24**). The life and trials of Joseph exemplifies integrity and honesty. In his life, one will see his character development as he is honest and a man of integrity. You will find that Joseph was not perfect, but loved God enough to obey Him and live according to the statues of God. He maintained his integrity, although he was a slave. It can be easy to forget Joseph was a slave, for he lived well and had great favor on his life.

At age 17, Joseph would report back to his father, the activities of his other 10 siblings. Genesis also records that Jacob loved Joseph more than his other brothers. Of course, this created a hatred for him by most of them. They knew their father, Jacob favored

Joseph. Joseph's father gave him a coat of many colors. During this time, Joseph had two dreams. In each dream others bowed to him (**Genesis 37:7-10**). Those others were his brothers in the dream. The interpretation angered his brothers. This act also brought rebuke from his father. The scripture states: that Jacob did not forget the dreams, although he rebuked Joseph (**Genesis 37: 1-11**). One could say that Joseph operated in spiritual pride as a youngster. But, Joseph possessed a measure of honesty and integrity. It is believed his father knew he would report the truth. As you study, the story of Joseph, you are reminded that children often do things in the absence of parents they would not do in their presence. Usually these are acts of disobedience. I would have been considered a "Joseph" in this area. I was obedient to my parents. I grew up with four siblings 2-3 years apart. We were together most of our time. We played and performed our chores together. Conflict was inevitable, and frequently arose. My mother would always ask me for the truth when issues arose. I could never lie to her, and she knew it. This did not gain approval from my siblings. Integrity and honesty were at work, although I was unaware. My siblings called me "goody two shoes." Although such words were hurtful, I always forgave them.

    Israel (or Jacob) sent Joseph again to observe his brothers feeding the flock away from home. His brothers left Shechem and traveled to Dothan. Joseph's brother saw him approaching them. They decided to kill him, calling him "the dreamer." His oldest brother, Reuben did not agree to kill him. Instead he suggested putting him in a pit with nothing to drink. Death still could occur. One brother determined killing Joseph would profit no one. The brothers agreed and sold Joseph to the Ishmaelite's who took him and sold him in Egypt as a slave. Joseph's coat of many colors was taken from him and covered with blood of a dead animal. This action would cause his father to think he was killed by an animal. Jacob was saddened when the news was given his son was dead, maybe killed by an animal. As Joseph was sold to the Egyptians, Potiphar the Egyptian officer of Pharaoh, was the recipient of the slave, Joseph (**Genesis 37:12-36**).

As mentioned, Joseph's siblings turned against him; as he was favored by his father. He had dreams that made him look great amongst his brethren. His brothers were jealous and conspired to kill him. He was sold to Egyptians, a form of persecution from his siblings. Little did they know it was a set-up by God for their future salvation and deliverance? Joseph's integrity and honest kept him in position to be used by God in the future of his family.

Joseph could have been bitter and unforgiving. He had ample opportunity to lie and cheat, and be revengeful. He was removed from all that he knew: his culture, his family, his friends, and his environment of worship. He could have chosen to forget God and his principles as issues arose in his life. Instead, he remained a person of honesty and integrity. He honored God in every situation by his actions. Did he think God had forsaken him? He chose to walk in integrity through his trials. He was jailed for lies spoken about his integrity. He would not sleep with boss' wife. His integrity was questioned, as he was judged wrongly. Joseph stood strong in his convictions. Joseph was trusted by his boss, but the wife spoke. She tried to lead him into sexual sins. He refused. He remained a man of integrity. Potiphar's wife came for him, he did not approach her. Joseph was imprisoned for his integrity, but rewarded by God through favor while in prison and after. He was given a leadership position in prison. His interpretation of dreams of his fellow prison mates, led him to a position of authority as he interpreted the dreams of the king (**Genesis 39-41:1-36**).

Being a person of honesty and integrity can bring persecution. Although, he was persecuted, Joseph continued to maintain the character of God. God blessed everything that Joseph did, as he was a man of integrity (**Genesis 39:2-6**). The integrity and honesty of God will strengthen you when tempted. You want the integrity of God to be a stronghold over your life. Let not trials and tribulations decrease your honesty and integrity. We will be tested. We must care for everything God has entrusted us with, even prayer. God is watching when we think not. These two will assist us in praying correctly for others. We will not gossip about those we pray and intercede for, God trusts you to receive information from Him to pray and keep unless he releases you to inform the person(s). Integrity of the heart will cause you to pray sincerely for your enemies. It will also cause you to pray and not judge while praying for others. You will love them with the love of Christ. Integrity in our personal life will travel with us into our prayer life.

I venture to say that with each new trial, Joseph learned something about himself and his God. I have often wondered if Joseph asked, why me God? The scriptures do not mention if he inquired this of the Lord. Perhaps, Joseph perceived his plight as an assignment that he must endure for His God. The scriptures do reveal his remembrance of the two prophetic dreams he had prior to being sold into slavery. Although his remembrance is mentioned, he did not charge this to his brothers. He realized he was in place for the famine to come. He would help his people. He saw the hidden blessing in his imprisonment.

As mentioned earlier, integrity in our personal life will travel with us into our prayer life. I am a single woman of God. Men of status and money have crossed my path numerous times. Twice I was offered a pathway of money through business that would have financially set me up for life. But what life would it have been? My relationship with God would have suffered. One person stated that I was not for sale. I praised God at that moment. Integrity and honesty would but all disappear. I politely said no. I was astonished at my quick reply. Thank God that He possessed my heart. His possession held me in a place of honesty and integrity. I informed each person that God is the center of my life. I also mentioned to God that this was tough, turning down the money. But, I am ever so grateful. At the time, of these occurrences; integrity and honesty did not enter my mind while in operation.

The integrity of Joseph in slavery was used by God to prepare a way for his people during times of distress. His honesty and integrity prevailed. Integrity is so important in our prayer life. As I have traveled in my prayer life, God has given me an assignment to pray for leaders. Some of these leaders acknowledged the assignment to their congregation. Ironically, others would often attempt to illicit information from me concerning that leader or ministry. My response was always that God had entrusted me with their concerns or prayer issues, and their concerns would remain confidential. The approval of God is foremost in my heart.

As aforementioned, integrity of the heart guides our actions. It will also gain us favor. The integrity of Joseph's heart gained him favor with his slave master, Potiphar. Joseph was given authority over all Potiphar's land, Egypt. Joseph most of all had the favor of God. A slave was given power to handle the affairs of the Egyptian king and land. Everything Joseph touched was blessed. Potiphar trusted Joseph. Again his honesty and integrity kept him. Someone was watching. What an honor given to Joseph (**Genesis 40:37-56**)!

However, obedient Joseph was, he had to yield to God's Word. His integrity caused him to be given authority over the land of Egypt. He prepared Egypt for seven years of famine as interpreted of Pharaoh's dream. He was able to serve his family in that manner. Grain and foods were available during the famine for his family (Genesis 42). The famine caused Joseph's brothers to seek grain in Egypt. His family was unaware that Joseph was in charge. Joseph recognized his brothers, they did not recognize him. At this point, Joseph could have been vindictive. He could had them murdered or imprisoned. He chose not to seek revenge, instead he forgave them. He asked if his father and younger brother were alive. He managed the situation to have his younger brother Benjamin brought to him. Many years had passed since his imprisonment, which worked to his advantage. Joseph was proved to be a man of honesty and integrity through his trials and wrong doings of others to him. He practiced the statues of God. We should take note and practice as Joseph did. His situations did not change the honesty and integrity of his heart (**Genesis 42-43**).

The Prayer

Lord, thank You for Your love, grace, and mercy. Father God, in the name of Your son, Jesus; forgive us of our sins. Forgive us of those sins that are known and unknown. Forgive us for not allowing You to tend to our hearts. Father, reveal to us any hidden things in our hearts. Forgive us Father, for any unresolved anger, bitterness, resentment, or unforgiveness. We repent of our sins. Show us the strategies to guard our hearts. We give You permission to change our hearts to look like Yours. Father, forgive us for not operating in honesty with hearts of integrity. We want hearts of integrity like Joseph. Help us to maintain honesty and integrity in church, outside of church, in stores, on the job, in offices, in the restaurant, in our homes, on the streets, social gatherings, and especially in our prayer lives. Help us to be mindful that You see us in all places. Guide us in all areas of our lives to bring You glory. We want your honesty and integrity to penetrate our hearts, mind, and soul. We will be flexible to You, and moved by Your Holy Spirit. Holy Spirit, prompt us when we are in disobedience. Father, increase Your will in our hearts. Build honesty and integrity in a greater measure for Your purposes in our lives and prayer life. Let us be pray-ers, intercessors, and warriors of integrity. I thank you for all these things in the name of Jesus.

DR. & PROPHETESS JACKIE MILLER

Dr. Miller was born in South Carolina. She was saved at the age of 10. Dr. Miller is Spirit filled and the founder and President of Epaphras Inc. The ministry is designed to teach and train God's people the truth through the Word of God and by His Spirit.

Dr. Miller has traveled and lived in different states including: South Carolina, North Carolina, Georgia, Texas, Maryland, and Washington, DC. She has been in ministry for twenty years, serving as pastor, associate pastor, and ministry leader. She received her Doctorate in Ministry from Family Bible College and Seminary. She received her Master's in Nursing from Morgan State University. She is an ordained pastor and prophet. Presently her ministry is a traveling school held for several months at a time. Classes taught include the prophetic ministry, prophetic gifting, ministry gifts, gifts of the Spirit, and gifts of God, as well as fruit of the Spirit. She is also utilized in the secular arena, educating nurses.

Daughters of Distinction

The Journey Through Prayer Concludes

Well, dear readers, we are back again with the second installment to our new series entitled "Seven Ingredients to an Effective Prayer Life." Through the reading of this book, you have discovered the final 2 ingredients which bring us to a total of seven ingredients that must be effective in your life. The sixth ingredient is "fruits of the spirit and the seventh ingredient are "honesty." Be confident (In GOD), faithful and attentive. We have found out that humility is favorable in God's eyes and is a must to be successful in this Christian walk. This leads me to the second ingredient, which is to "seek." Did you notice the order? One must be humble first postured correctly in order to seek God and be effective. I know you discovered how to properly seek the Father after you entered into the correct posture of humility. The third ingredient is true repentance. You discovered what true repentance really means and how it is to be applied daily in our lives. The fourth ingredient is righteousness. We must always be in right standing with God. The authors shared their experiences in how to obtain and maintain a life of righteousness. The fifth ingredient is holiness. This is where we get nervous. It's not about your outward appearance but your inward parts which truly matters to God. Embrace yourself living a life of holiness which can be obtained. In this book you will learn about our final two ingredients. The Sixth ingredient is "fruits of the spirit." You will learn the reason we must possess each fruit of the spirit not just one. All are needed to be effective in life and through prayer. They are key attributes of Godly character. It is a MUST! The seventh and final ingredient is honesty. We must remain honest with God at all times especially in prayer. Be honest about your struggles and disappointments. God honors honesty. Be transport with the Father at all times. The authors truly express the importance of honesty and the fruits of the spirit. I pray that as we journeyed together that our faith was renewed and our pray life was increased with passion and fire. The journey through prayer is now complete. This has been awesome journey we embarked upon. I'll see you soon on our next journey.

I love you more than you will ever know
Trena

THE VISIONARY

Apostle Trena Stephenson is a gifted preacher, teacher, worship leader, author, playwright, entrepreneur and intercessor. Apostle Trena developed and formed Daughters of Distinction LLC in 2008, based off of her passion for writing and helping others fulfill their passions, as well. Daughters of Distinction was designed to impact this world with the gospel of Jesus Christ through books, television and radio ventures. She is a visionary, a woman of great faith, compassion, and integrity. She has been a guest speaker on several programs including: "The Wenda Royster Show," Radio One, Rejoice TV Network, TBN, and Preach the Word Network. In April 2008, Apostle Stephenson became the executive producer and creative director for Daughters of Distinction TV which houses two shows "Daughters of Distinction Live" and "Let's Talk", a new show which launched in April 2011. Both shows air on Rejoice TV Network in Maryland and District Columbia. In May 7, 2011, Apostle Stephenson launched The Fullness of God Radio Broadcast airing in Alabama, Pennsylvania, Florida, Louisiana, South Carolina, North Carolina and Georgia. In September 2010, Apostle Trena also launched Soar Magazine an online magazine to empower and

Daughters of Distinction

encourage the people of God. In 2013, Apostle Stephenson launched Daily Living TV Network where she is co-founder and CEO. When God opens the door for Apostle Stephenson, she walks through it under the Anointing of the Holy Spirit with the purpose of leading someone to Christ.

To learn more about this awesome woman of God, log onto: www.dofdllc.com, www.soarmagazine.info and www.dailylivingnetwork.net.

RELEASES FROM DAUGHTERS OF DISTINCTION

7 Ingredients to an Effective Prayer Life

Volume 1-2

Volume 3-5

To learn more about the services and upcoming releases go to
www.dofdllc.com
Find us on the web @ www. soarmagazine.info &
www.wofgod.org

REFERENCES

1. "love." Merriam Webster.com. Merriam-Webster. 9 July. 2013. <http://www.merriam-webster.com/dictionary/love>.
2. "joy." Webster's New World College Dictionary. 4th edition. 1999
3. "persona." Merriam-Webster.com. 2013. http://www.merriam-webster.com/dictionary/persona (25 June 2013).
4. Omartian, Stormie. The Power of a Praying Woman. Eugene: Harvest House Publishers, 2002.
5. Guyon, Jeanne. Experiencing God Through Prayer. New Kensington: Whitaker House, 1984.
6. Ibid
7. MacArthur, John. Grace to You (15 Oct. 2004)
8. Warren, Richard. The Purpose-driven Life: What on Earth Am I Here For? Grand Rapids, MI: Zondervan, 2002.
9. Unknown. "The Seed of Honesty." Web log post. AcademicTips.org. N.p., 28 June 2012. Web. 7 July 2013. <http://academictips.org/blogs/the-seed-of-honesty/>.
10. "honesty." Merriam Webster.com. Merriam-Webster. 9 July. 2013. <http://www.merriam-webster.com/dictionary/honesty>.
11. "honesty." Microsoft Encarta World English Dictionary. 2009. U.S. version on CD, developed by Microsoft
12. "honest." Merriam Webster.com. Merriam-Webster. 27 February. 2013. <http://www.merriam-webster.com/dictionary/honest>.
13. "honesty." Merriam Webster.com. Merriam-Webster. 27 February. 2013. <http://www.merriam-webster.com/dictionary/honesty>.
14. Ibid
15. "Semnotes." James Strong Hebrew Dictionary. Nashville: Thomas Nelson, 2010.
16. "integrity." Webster's New World College Dictionary. 4th edition. 1999

www.ingramcontent.com/pod-product-compliance
Lightning Source LLC
Chambersburg PA
CBHW070457100426
42743CB00010B/1664